JavaScript™

P H R A S E B O O K

ESSENTIAL CODE AND COMMANDS

Christian Wenz

DEVELOPER'S
LIBRARY

Sams Publishing, 800 East 96th Street, Indianapolis, Indiana 46240 USA

International Standard Book Number: 0-672-32880-1

Library of Congress Catalog Card Number: 2005909314

Printed in the United States of America

First Printing: August 2006

09   08   07   4   3

Trademarks

Warning and Disclaimer

Bulk Sales

Sams Publishing offers excellent discounts on this book when ordered in quantity for bulk purchases or special sales. For more information, please contact

U.S. Corporate and Government Sales
1-800-382-3419
corpsales@pearsontechgroup.com

For sales outside of the U.S., please contact

International Sales
international@pearsoned.com

The Safari® Enabled icon on the cover of your favorite technology book means the book is available through Safari Bookshelf. When you buy this book, you get free access to the online edition for 45 days. Safari Bookshelf is an electronic reference library that lets you easily search thousands of technical books, find code samples, download chapters, and access technical information whenever and wherever you need it.

To gain 45-day Safari Enabled access to this book:

- Go to http://www.samspublishing.com/safarienabled
- Complete the brief registration form
- Enter the coupon code **JTIM-HPQH-7MXN-BXHL-QRK1**

If you have difficulty registering on Safari Bookshelf or accessing the online edition, please e-mail customer-service@safaribooksonline.com.

Acquisitions and Development Editor	Project Editor	Proofreader	Book Designer
Damon Jordan	Lori Lyons	Linda K. Seifert	Gary Adair
Managing Editor	**Copy Editor**	**Technical Editor**	**Page Layout**
Gina Kanouse	Cheri Clark	Phil Ballard	Nonie Ratcliff
	Indexer	**Publishing Coordinator**	
	Erica Millen	Karen Opal	

Table of Contents

Contents

Contents

Contents

About the Author

Christian Wenz is a professional phrasemonger, author, trainer, and consultant with a focus on web technologies. He has written or cowritten more than four dozen books. He frequently contributes articles to renowned IT magazines and speaks at conferences around the globe. Christian contributes to several PHP packages in the PEAR repository and also maintains one Perl CPAN module. He holds a degree ("Diplom") in Computer Sciences from Technical University of Munich and lives and works in Munich, Germany. He also is Europe's very first Zend Certified Professional and founding principal at the PHP Security Consortium.

We Want to Hear from You!

As the reader of this book, *you* are our most important critic and commentator. We value your opinion and want to know what we're doing right, what we could do better, what areas you'd like to see us publish in, and any other words of wisdom you're willing to pass our way.

You can email or write me directly to let me know what you did or didn't like about this book—as well as what we can do to make our books stronger.

Please note that I cannot help you with technical problems related to the topic of this book, and that due to the high volume of mail I receive, I might not be able to reply to every message.

When you write, please be sure to include this book's title and author as well as your name and phone or email address. I will carefully review your comments and share them with the author and editors who worked on the book.

E-mail: webdev@samspublishing.com

Mail: Mark Taber
          Associate Publisher
          Sams Publishing
          800 East 96th Street
          Indianapolis, IN 46240 USA

Reader Services

Visit our website and register this book at www.samspublishing.com/register for convenient access to any updates, downloads, or errata that might be available for this book.

Introduction

Back in 1999, I wrote a book on JavaScript. At the beginning, it sold really great, and then sales started to decrease a little bit. It still sold well enough to reach seven editions by this fall, but there was a subtle decline in copies nevertheless.

However, all of this changed drastically at the end of last year—sales went up considerably, as did sales of other titles in the same segment. But how come? One of the reasons is AJAX. The technology itself is not new, but the term is. In February 2005, Jesse James Garrett coined the acronym, and since then, the whole web world seems to have gone crazy. And although AJAX can be explained in a couple of minutes actually, it requires a good knowledge of various aspects of JavaScript. This explains the growing demand for advanced JavaScript content, and also led to the writing of the *JavaScript Phrasebook*.

When we (Damon Jordan, Mark Taber, and I) created the book series in 2005, we wanted to create a kind of pimped-up version of language phrasebooks: Common sentences and expressions are translated into a foreign language—into JavaScript, of course. However, unlike in a regular phrasebook, you will also get explanations alongside the code. Without it, the potential for embarrassing situations is quite high, in any language.

This book is no introduction to JavaScript. Elementary JavaScript features are covered, but we tried to put a great emphasis on intermediary and advanced material as well. The idea behind this phrasebook is that especially if your JavaScript knowledge is rusty, you will find common problems and solutions in this book. So use this book as a reference guide to quickly overcome issues you are facing during development. And explore the book to find some JavaScript features you may not have thought about before.

This book is no cookbook with long and inflexible solutions to short problems. The idea was to keep the code snippets as concise as possible so that the approach can be demonstrated; this enables you to adapt the presented technique to your own applications and your specific scenario. In order to make this possible, only the code elements that are vital for the samples to run are shown in this book. Usually, the code consists only of `<script>` elements and some other HTML tags to tie everything together. A modern web application should at least try to be XHTML-compliant, but this is not the focus of the elements of this book.

We took great care to make the code work on as many browsers as possible. And while Internet Explorer and the various Mozilla flavors (including Firefox) dominate the market, Opera, Safari, and Konqueror also have their share in it. So while the focus of the phrases lies on the first two browser types, incompatibilities or caveats regarding the smaller browsers are noted where appropriate. Speaking of market shares: Only browsers that are still relevant as of today are covered; therefore, Netscape 4 and Internet Explorer 4 are not mentioned at all.

Code samples to this title and updates can be found at http://javascript.phrasebook.org/. Most listings have the associated filename with them, so you can easily find the right file(s) for each phrase. If you have any feedback or have found an error, please let me know! If a phrase you were hoping to find is missing, please let me know. If you think that it should appear in upcoming editions of the book, I'd also appreciate if you'd nominate another phrase that you feel is super-fluous. (These books are small, and there's only so much space.) The list of potential phrases was much longer than what you are holding in your hands now, so we went through a painful process of eliminating content—and hope that the selection is to your liking.

Finally, thank you to a bunch of people who helped make this phrasebook more useful than the famous dictionary in the Monty Python sketch that mapped innocent expressions to vulgar translations: Shelley Johnston set this project up and convinced me to do the original phrasebook (*PHP Phrasebook*). Damon Jordan also worked on the *PHP Phrasebook* and served as the editor for this title. Phil Ballard tech-edited this book. Thanks for all your hard work on this!

Also, thanks to Judith Stevens-Lemoine, who has been editing "my other" JavaScript book since 1999. I'd like to thank her for giving me permission to write this phrasebook. Looking forward to the eighth edition!

Your personal phrasemonger,
Christian Wenz

1

JavaScript Basics

This chapter covers some basics regarding JavaScript. It does not explicitly cover the language syntax itself—this is covered in enough tutorials and books and does not fit into the phrasebook concept. However, fundamentals such as putting JavaScript code in a page are explained in detail. Also, a bit of JavaScript history and browser war stories are used to get you ready for the phrases to come in the following chapters.

Understanding JavaScript (and Its History)

JavaScript is a client-side scripting language—that means a language that runs on the client side, within a web browser. (JavaScript can also be used on the server side and otherwise outside a browser, but this is not of interest for the purpose of this book.) If the browser supports the language, JavaScript grants access to the current page and lets the script determine properties of the client, redirect the user to another page, access cookies, and do much more.

The birth of JavaScript was in September 1995, when version 2.0 of the Netscape browser was released, the first version to come with the scripting language. Back then, the name of the language was first Mocha and then, when released, LiveScript; but Netscape made a marketing deal with Sun (creator of Java) and renamed the language to JavaScript in December of that year.

The concept received a large following, so Microsoft included JavaScript support from Internet Explorer version 3 onward (mid-1996). For legal reasons, the Microsoft flavor of the language was called JScript. JScript was more or less compatible with JavaScript, but started to include additional, IE-only features (that—apart from some exceptions—never really caught on).

In 1997, the standard ECMAScript (ECMA-262) was published; JavaScript is therefore the first implementation of that standard. The standard itself specifies only the language, but not features of the surrounding hosts (for instance, how to access the current browser window or open a new one). ECMAScript became an ISO norm in 1998.

Around 1997 or 1998, the browser war between Netscape and Microsoft reached a climax, with both vendors adding new, incompatible functionality to version 5 of their browsers. The rest is history: Netscape scrapped the idea of releasing browser version 5 and decided to start all over with Netscape 6, which helped Internet Explorer to expand its market share to over 90%. It took the then-founded Mozilla project several years to come to life again. The very popular Firefox browser was based on Mozilla and started to take market share away from Microsoft.

From the JavaScript point of view, not very much has happened in the past few years. Firefox 1.5, which was released in late 2005, supports the new JavaScript version 1.6, but changes are rather minimal—and Internet Explorer is far away from supporting that. But with Internet Explorer 7 and Firefox 2.0 in the foreseeable future (and both already available in a preview version), it's an interesting time for a web developer.

Other browsers, by the way, support JavaScript as well. Differences are subtle, but still can be extremely annoying when one is developing a browser-agnostic web application. Among the browsers that currently support JavaScript are the following:

- Internet Explorer
- Mozilla and all derivates (Firefox, Epiphany, Camino, Galeon, and so on)
- Opera
- Konqueror
- Safari

Setting Up a Test System

As just mentioned, several browsers do support JavaScript. Usually, you have to support most of them. For instance, the website http://marketshare.hitslink. com/report.aspx?qprid=3 shows that in March 2006, Internet Explorer and Firefox together accounted for close to 95% of the browser market share, with Safari following (slightly over 3%). Netscape browsers held about 1% and Opera had about half a percent, which was about the same as all other browsers (including Konqueror) had together.

So what is the best strategy to test a website on as many systems as possible, but with the least effort?

It really depends on what the audience of your website is. If you have a really high portion of Mac users, you do have to do extensive testing with the Safari browser, since this browser comes by default with recent versions of Mac OS X.

No matter which kind of website you are using, Internet Explorer still has a very strong market share, even on more open-source–centric websites. Therefore, you need Internet Explorer, and thus a Windows system is required for testing (or at least something like Virtual PC or VMware with a Windows virtual machine). All Mozilla browsers share the same codebase for rendering and also for JavaScript, and therefore it does not really matter which platform you are using (albeit there are some minimal differences). So you could, for instance, use Firefox on the same Windows machine your Internet Explorer installation resides on.

Opera runs under Windows (and a couple of other systems, including Linux and Mac) as well, so the Windows partition gets one more browser.

The only two major browsers now remaining are Safari and Konqueror, the latter one being the default browser when the KDE window manager is used. Luckily, they both share the same codebase, more or less: Safari uses the KHTML engine that is the heart of the Konqueror rendering. Therefore, two options come to mind:

- Set up a Linux box (or a Linux virtual machine) with KDE and Konqueror.

- Set up a Mac system (or buy an Intel Mac with BootCamp to dual-boot Windows and OS X)

This should at least give you a good system to start testing with. The larger the website gets, the more important it is to support as many target systems as possible; from a certain point on, you will have no other choice than to install and test on every browser you want to support.

Regarding Internet Explorer, currently version 6 is the major one, whereas version 5.x is almost extinct and versions 4 and earlier are long gone. Therefore, just testing in IE 6 is acceptable in most cases. Having different versions to test is of course quite desirable, but usually requires one Windows system each, since only one IE installation per system is allowed.

By accident, a solution for parallel installing several IE versions was found. You can find the original description of that on http://labs.insert-title.com/labs/Multiple-IEs-in-Windows_article795.aspx and more information at http://www.positioniseverything.net/articles/multiIE.html.

Finally, make sure that you test your website(s) with JavaScript both enabled and disabled in browsers.

Configuring Web Browsers

By default, most JavaScript-capable web browsers do support JavaScript. Actually, the very first Netscape version to support JavaScript did not even have a feature to turn it off!

However, JavaScript can be turned off, so you should find out how to simulate that (and how to instruct users just to turn it on). This depends not only on the browsers used, but sometimes also on the browser version. In Firefox 1.5 browsers, JavaScript can be enabled using Tools, Options, Content, Enable JavaScript. In Internet Explorer 6 you have to dig a little bit deeper: Tools, Internet Options, Security, Internet Zone, Custom Level, Scripting, Active Scripting, Enable.

TIP: Internet Explorer versions 6.0 and 7.0 (on Windows XP, 2003, and Vista only) has a security feature that blocks JavaScript running on local pages (see Figure 1.1). This is quite useful actually, but it can be quite annoying when you're testing an application. There are two workarounds: Either use a local web server to test your application, or just deactivate the error message, by choosing Tools, Internet Options, Advanced, Security, Allow active content to run in files from My Computer.

Figure 1.1   A rather annoying error message with JavaScript on local pages.

Including JavaScript Code

```
<script type="text/javascript">
  window.alert("Welcome to JavaScript!");
</script>
```

JavaScript code can come in two ways: either embedded into an HTML page, or in an external file. The most common way to include JavaScript code is to use the `<script>` element. You can place this element anywhere, and the code is then executed after this part of the HTML page has been loaded and parsed. The preceding code (file `script.html` in the download archive) opens a modal window and prints some rather simple text.

The `type` attribute provides the MIME type for JavaScript. Previously, `language="JavaScript"` was used; however, since that was not standardized, it is considered best practice to use `type` and the MIME type instead. In this book, we follow the approach many websites are using nowadays: Both `type` and `language` are used.

Also, back in the old days, it was possible to target a script to a specific version number of JavaScript, like this:

```
<script language="JavaScript1.6">
  window.alert("Only with JavaScript 1.6!");
</script>
```

However, this is almost never used now. First of all, implementation of this feature has been quite buggy in browsers, and there are better ways of testing a browser's JavaScript capabilities.

NOTE: In some old tutorials you will find the advice to use HTML comments in the following fashion:

```
<script language="JavaScript"><!--
  // ...
//--></script>
```

NOTE: This was previously used to cope with browsers that did not know anything of JavaScript. However, even browsers that do not support JavaScript know about the `<script>` element and know to ignore it (including its contents). Therefore, these HTML comments are not necessary any longer.

Using External JavaScript Files

```
<script language="JavaScript" type="text/javascript"
   src="script.js"></script>
```

Especially when you are reusing JavaScript code on your website, an external JavaScript file (or several files) comes in handy. This external file contains only the JavaScript code, no `<script>` elements. A `<script>` element is, however, used to load the external file, as can be seen from the previous listing (file `scriptsrc.html`). The `src` attribute holds the URL of the external script; absolute URLs (and, therefore, remote servers) are also possible.

WARNING: Note that the code in the external file is available only after the external file has been fully loaded. So especially when calling functionality in the external file from the local page, keep in mind that the external file may not be available yet.

Dynamically Loading JavaScript Files

```
var s = document.createElement("script");
```

Sometimes it is necessary to load JavaScript code on demand, while a site is running. For instance, depending on user input, a specific external JavaScript file must be loaded.

One attempt is to use document.write() to dynamically add a new <script> element to the page. However, this fails with some browsers and also is not considered good style. A much better solution is to use DOM. First, you create a new <script> element and set the appropriate attributes. Then, you add this element to the page's DOM (see Chapter 5). Usually, the code is put in the <head> section of the page. The following listing shows the complete code; note that there actually is a <head> element so that the code works. Figure 1.2 shows the result of this code.

```
<html>
<head>
<title>JavaScript</title>
</head>
<body>
<script language="JavaScript"
  type="text/javascript">
  var s = document.createElement("script");
  s.setAttribute("type", "text/javascript");
  s.setAttribute("language", "JavaScript");
  s.setAttribute("src", "script.js");
  document.getElementsByTagName("head")[0]
➥.appendChild(s);
```

```
</script>
</body>
</html>
```

Dynamically Adding a Script (scriptdynamic.html)

Figure 1.2   The modal window comes from the
external file that was dynamically loaded.

Using JavaScript Pseudo URLs

```
<a href="javascript:window.alert('Welcome to
JavaScript!');">click here for a surprise</a>
```

Another way to call JavaScript code is to use a pseudo
URL. When a URL that begins with javascript: is
loaded, the code behind that is executed, as can be
seen in the preceding code (file url.html).

There are several ways to use such a URL—in the
form of an image, a link, or a CSS style—but usually
it's the link you will want to use. Note, however, that
such a link obviously works only with a browser that
supports JavaScript and has it activated.

> **WARNING:** When the code after the `javascript:` URL
> prefix returns something, the result is printed to the
> screen. Usually, this is not desirable. You can use the
> special JavaScript function `void()` to avoid this:
>
> `javascript:void(code_that_would_return_something());`

Executing JavaScript with Event Handlers

```
<body onload="showText();">
```

The third way to execute JavaScript code (the first two
ones being `<script>` elements and `javascript:` pseudo
URLs) is via en event handler. Most HTML elements
support a few events; for instance, the `<body>` tag supports the load element. Using the `on` prefix, code can
be attached to this event (more options are covered in
Chapter 6, "OOP and Events"). Therefore, the following code runs the `showText()` function after the document has been fully loaded (with respect to the
HTML markup of the page, not images or other
external data):

```
<html>
<head>
<title>JavaScript</title>
<script language="JavaScript"
  type="text/javascript">
  function showText() {
    window.alert("Welcome to JavaScript!");
  }
</script>
</head>
```

```
<body onload="showText();">
</body>
</html>
```

Using a JavaScript Event Handler (event.html)

WARNING: It is a common misconception that the
`javascript:` URL prefix must be used with event handlers,
in the following fashion:

```
<body onload="javascript:showText();">
```

However, this is completely bogus—what else if not
JavaScript code could be the value of an event handler
attribute? Therefore, omit the `javascript:` and just provide the code to be executed when the associated event
is fired.

Coping with Browsers without JavaScript

```
<script type="text/javascript">
  document.write("Welcome to JavaScript!");
</script>
<noscript>
  Welcome to plain HTML!
</noscript>
```

According to recent surveys, up to 10% of users have
JavaScript disabled, due to company policies, fear of
browser security vulnerabilities, and other reasons.
Therefore, you do have to make sure that your website
can be used without JavaScript, as well.

One way to achieve this is to use the <noscript> element. Browsers with activated JavaScript ignore this element and its contents, whereas browsers without JavaScript show the element's contents. The preceding code (file noscript.html) generates the output shown in Figure 1.3 when a non-JavaScript browser (like the text browser Lynx) is used; Figure 1.4 shows a browser that supports the scripting language.

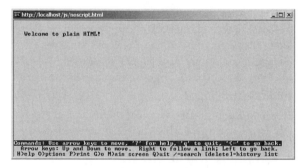

Figure 1.3   The preceding code in a browser without JavaScript.

Figure 1.4   The preceding code in a browser with JavaScript.

When JavaScript is used together with links, the following does not work fully as expected:

```
<a href="#" onclick="window.alert('Welcome to
    JavaScript!'); ">click here</a>
```

At first sight, we did everything right: Users with JavaScript get the modal window, users without JavaScript just click on a link to an empty text label; so nothing unexpected happens.

However, there is one little disadvantage: After the JavaScript link is clicked, a JavaScript-enabled browser shows the window but then still follows the link. Usually, that does not have an effect, but the browser scrolls to the top of the page because the text label has not been found.

To avoid this, just make sure that the code in the event handler returns `false`. This cancels all other effects the current event may have; in this case, the link will not be followed:

```
<a href="#" onclick="window.alert('Welcome to
    JavaScript!'); return false;">click here</a>
```

Avoiding that JavaScript-Enabled Browsers Still Follow the Link (link.html)

2

Common Phrases

There are some recurring JavaScript tasks you need to perform almost daily. They build the foundation of many JavaScript applications and do not fit into any specific category. Therefore, this chapter starts with a collection of common problems—and solutions.

Detecting the Browser Type

```
window.alert(navigator.appName);
```

Although browsers' implementations of JavaScript are quite compatible with each other nowadays (especially when compared with the situation during the browser war at the end of the 1990s), detecting the browser type is a vital part of the JavaScript developer's toolbox.

The navigator JavaScript object provides browser information. Most useful, but also sometimes challenging to parse, is its userAgent property, which contains the complete browser identification string that is also sent in the HTTP User-Agent header with each request.

To just determine the browser type, the `appName` property suffices, as the preceding code shows. Table 2.1 contains the `appName` values for the most relevant browsers.

Table 2.1   The appName Values for Various Browsers

Browser	appName
Internet Explorer	`Microsoft Internet Explorer`
Mozilla Browsers	`Netscape`
Konqueror (KDE)	`Konqueror`
Apple Safari	`Netscape`
Opera Browser	`Opera`

So as you can see, the Safari browser returns the incorrect name. To mitigate this effect, you can search `navigator.userAgent` for certain browser types. Since the Opera browser can identify itself as another browser (but then still mentions `"Opera"` in `navigator.userAgent`), this browser has to be checked first.

```
<script language="JavaScript"
  type="text/javascript">
var uA = navigator.userAgent;
var browserType = "unknown";
if (uA.indexOf("Opera") > -1) {
  browserType = "Opera";
} else if (uA.indexOf("Safari") > -1) {
  browserType = "Safari";
} else if (uA.indexOf("Konqueror") > -1) {
  browserType = "Konqueror";
} else if (uA.indexOf("Gecko") > -1) {
  browserType = "Mozilla";
} else if (uA.indexOf("MSIE") > -1) {
```

```
  browserType = "Internet Explorer";
}
window.alert(browserType);
</script>
```

Determining the Browser Type (browser.html)

With a little bit of effort, this script can be extended to distinguish the Mozilla derivatives (Firefox, Epiphany, Galeon, Camino, SeaMonkey, and so on) as well.

Detecting the Browser Version Number

To determine the browser's version number, several approaches exist. Most of the time, you have a look at navigator.userAgent, which can look like the following:

```
Mozilla/5.0 (Windows; U; Windows NT 5.1; en;
    rv:1.8.0.3) Gecko/20060426 Firefox 1.5.0.3
Mozilla/5.0 (Windows; U; Windows NT 5.1; en-US;
    rv:1.4) Gecko/20030619 Netscape/7.1 (ax)
Mozilla/4.0 (compatible; MSIE 6.0; Windows NT 5.1;
    SV1; .NET CLR 1.0.3705; .NET CLR 1.1.4322;
    .NET CLR 2.0.50727)
Mozilla/5.0 (compatible; Konqueror/3.4; FreeBSD)
    KHTML/3.4.2 (like Gecko)
Mozilla/5.0 (Macintosh; U; Intel Mac OS X; en)
    AppleWebKit/418 (KHTML, like Gecko)
    Safari/417.9.3
Mozilla/5.0 (Macintosh; U; PPC Mac OS X; en)
    AppleWebKit/312.8 (KHTML, like Gecko)
    Safari/312.6
Opera/9.00 (Windows NT 5.1; U; en)
Mozilla/4.0 (compatible; MSIE 6.0; Windows NT 5.1;
    en) Opera 9.00
```

So as you can see, depending on the browser type, the version number is buried somewhere else within the value of `navigator.userAgent`. Therefore, it is a tedious task to cover all possible browsers and to keep on track with new methods. However, there are some web resources that implement a quite decent browser detection. You will find more documentation and code on these websites:

- http://www.webreference.com/tools/browser/ javascript.html

- http://gemal.dk/browserspy/basic.html

Checking Browser Capabilities

```
if (document.getElementById) {
  // ...
```

As you could see from the previous examples, relying on browser version numbers is not only difficult, but also not future-proof. A much better way to check whether a browser supports the features your application requires is to specifically check for the support of the special objects.

For instance, to use DOM (see Chapter 5, "DOM and DHTML"), you might want to try the preceding code. If the `getElementById()` method is implemented, `document.getElementById` (without parentheses) returns a reference to the function. If used within a condition, this evaluates to `true`. Therefore, the associated code is executed.

Another example: Internet Explorer supports ActiveX objects for certain applications, for instance XML support. However, only the Windows versions of IE know ActiveX—the Mac versions don't. So specifically checking for Internet Explorer creates problems for Mac users. If you specifically check for the ActiveX support, you avoid these issues:

```
if (window.ActiveXObject) {
  // ...
}
```

Preventing Caching

```
document.write("<img src=\"image.png?" +
  Math.random() + "\" />");
```

Using server-side headers, the caching of dynamic content–like images and also HTML pages can be avoided. However, this approach is not bulletproof, since some browsers or proxy servers can ignore these settings. A technique that always works is appending a meaningless query string parameter to the URL, as in the following fashion: `Math.random()` returns a random number between 0 and 1, for instance `0.1296601696732852`. Appending this to an image usually does not change the data sent from the server, but it is a completely new request for the browser. Therefore, the image (or other data) is not cached.

Redirecting the Browser

```
location.href = "newPage.html";
```

The `location.href` property allows read and write access to the URL of the current page. Consequence:

Setting location.href to another value redirects the browser, which then loads the new page, as the preceding code shows.

TIP: This can also be done by HTML means:

```
<meta http-equiv="Refresh" content="X; URL=Y" />
```

The placeholder X stands for the number of seconds to wait until the new page is loaded; Y denotes the new URL.

The previous page then lands in the history of the browser. If you however want to replace the old page in the browser history (to make the back button not work as expected here), use the location.replace() method:

```
location.replace("newPage.html");
```

Reloading the Page

```
location.reload();
```

The reload() method of the location object reloads the current page, which is equivalent to location.href = location.href. If you provide true as a parameter, caching is disabled and the browser does a "hard" reload from the server. However, this is also not bulletproof, since there could be a proxy server in between that could have a cached copy of the requested page. So you could use the "Preventing Caching" phrase technique from this chapter instead:

```
location.search = "?" + Math.random();
```

This changes the query string (location.search) of the current page, effectively reloading the URL reload() .

Creating a Random Number

```
var rand = min + Math.floor((max - min + 1) *
  Math.random());
```

The `random()` method of the `Math` object calculates a pseudo-random number between 0 and 1 (excluding). However, usually you are interested in a random number between, say, 1 and 10. With a small mathematical calculation, this can be achieved. For the example, multiply the result of `Math.random()` by 10, effectively generating a number between 0 and 10 (excluding). If you then round this value, you get an integral number between 0 and 9 (including). Adding 1 leads to a number between 1 and 10.

The preceding code generalizes this and creates a number between `min` and `max`.

Date and Time Information

```
var d = new Date();
var mdy = (d.getMonth()+1) + "/" + d.getDate() +
```

JavaScript's `Date` object provides access to the current date and is also capable of doing certain Date calculations (using the epoch value, the number of milliseconds since January 1, 1970). Table 2.2 contains the most important methods of the `Date` class. The preceding code creates a date in the format `month/day/year`.

Table 2.2   Some Date Properties

Method	Description
getDate()	Day of the month
getFullYear()	Four-digit year
getHours()	Hours
getMinutes()	Minutes
getMonth()	Month minus 1 (!)
getSeconds()	Seconds
getTime()	Epoch value
toString()	String representation
toUTCString()	UTC string representation

Understanding Regular Expressions

Regular expressions are, to put it simply, patterns that can be matched with strings. A pattern in a regular expression contains a string that can be searched for in a larger string. However, this can also be done (faster) using indexOf(). The advantage of regular expressions is that some special features such as wildcards are available. Table 2.3 shows some special characters and their meanings.

Table 2.3   Special Characters in Regular Expressions

Special Character	Description	Example
^	Beginning of the string	^a means a string that starts with a
$	End of the string	a$ means a string that ends with a

Special Character	Description	Example
?	0 or 1 times (refers to the previous character or expression)	ab? means a or ab
*	0 or more times (refers to the previous character or expression)	ab* means a or ab or abb or...
+	1 or more times (refers to the previous character or expression)	ab+ means ab or abb or abbb or...
[...]	Alternative characters	PHP[45] means PHP4 or PHP5
- (used within square brackets)	A sequence of values	ECMAScript [3-5] means ECMAScript 3 or ECMAScript 4 or ECMAScript 5
^ (used within square brackets)	Does match anything but the following characters	[^A-C] means D or E or F or...
|	Alternative patterns	ECMAScript 3|ECMAScript 4 means ECMAScript 3 or ECMAScript 4, as does ECMAScript (3|4)
(...)	Defines a subpattern	(a)(b) means ab, but with two subpatterns (a and b)

Table 2.3   Continued

Special Character	Description	Example
.	Any character	. means a, b, c, 0, 1, 2, \$, ^,...
{min, max}	Minimum and maximum number of occurrences; if either min or max is omitted, it means 0 or infinite	a{1,3} means a, aa, or aaa. a{,3} means empty string, a, aa, or aaa. a{1,} means a, aa, aaa,...
\	escapes the following character	\. stands for .

Other special characters and expressions are available, for instance, a character that refers to a digit (\d).

Searching with Regular Expressions

```
zip.test("Indianapolis, IN 46240");
```

Defining a regular expression in JavaScript can be done in two ways:

- var zip = new RegEx("\\d{5}");
- var zip = /\d{5}/;

There is no functional difference between the two approaches; you just have to take character escaping into account. Then, the test() method of the expression checks whether a string contains the regular expression:

```
var found = zip.test("Indianapolis, IN 46240");
//true
```

If you are interested in the actual match, use the exec() function. The method returns an array. Its first array element is the whole match, and the next elements are all submatches (if parentheses are used in the regular expression).

```
var matches = zip.exec("Indianapolis, IN 46240");
// ["46240"]
```

TIP: The method match() returns all matches; exec() returns only the current match, usually the first one. However, if you call exec() multiple times, all matches are returned.

Replacing Text

```
var address = /(\w+), ([A-Z]{2}) (\d{5})/;
var sams = "Indianapolis, IN 46240";
var result = sams.replace(address, "$3 $1, $2");
```

The replace() method every JavaScript string supports can replace text. It searches for a regular expression and replaces the match with another string. Within this replacement string, you can back-reference submatches. $0 points to the first match, $1 references the first submatch (within parentheses), $2 the second submatch, and so on. The preceding code searches for the city, state, and zip code elements and then rearranges them. The result is "46240 Indianapolis, IN".

Navigating within the Browser's History

```
window.history.back();
window.history.forward();
```

The browser history is represented by the history object (a property of the window object) and contains a list of web pages visited prior to (and, if available, after) the current page. And although it is technically possible to move a couple of elements within the history, security constraints leave only one viable way: going one page back and one page forward. The following two methods implement that:

- back() moves to the previous page in the history (like the back button does).

- forward() moves to the next page in the history (like the forward button does).

Displaying the Modification Date of the Page

```
document.write(document.lastModified);
```

Whenever a web server sends a resource to the client, it also sends the date the document was modified the last time. Usually, the web server takes this information from the file system, but this header can also be modified or just not sent. But anyway, you can use this information, for instance as shown in the preceding code. Therefore, you can have a more or less realistic modification date on your page.

Retrieving GET Parameters

```
var ls = location.search.substring(1);
var namevalue = ls.split("&");
```

Usually, GET information is evaluated on the server side, but JavaScript does also have access to this information via its location.search property. However, the data there is in name-value pairs. The following code decodes this data by using the JavaScript split() method. The resulting associative array is then shown, just to prove that it works as expected; see Figure 2.1 for the output.

```
<script language="JavaScript"
  type="text/javascript">
var getdata = [];
if (location.search.length > 1) {
  var ls = location.search.substring(1);
  var namevalue = ls.split("&");
  for (var i=0; i<namevalue.length; i++) {
    var data = namevalue[i].split("=");
    getdata[data[0]] = data[1];
  }
}

var s = "";
for (var el in getdata) {
  s += el + ": " + getdata… + "\n";
}
alert(s);
</script>
```

Parsing the Query String (querystring.html)

Figure 2.1 The data from the query string
is parsed and shown.

Asking for User Confirmation

```
<a href="anyPage.html"
  onclick="return window.confirm('Do you really want
to do this?');">Click here</a>
```

JavaScript offers limited support for modal windows.
The window.alert() method is fairly common, but
there are other options as well. With window.confirm(),
the user is presented with a Yes/No window. If Yes is
clicked, window.confirm() returns true; otherwise,
false. The preceding code (file confirm.html) uses this
as the return value for a link, so if No is clicked, the
link is not followed.

WARNING: Note that this dialog is translated by browsers,
so you should avoid text like "Click Yes to..." since users
with a non-English system do not have a Yes button.

Asking for User Data

```
var name =
  window.prompt("Enter your name!", "<Your name>");
```

The window.prompt() method allows users to enter text into a single-line text field (see Figure 2.2). This information is the return value of the method call and can be further used in the script.

```
<script language="JavaScript"
  type="text/javascript">
var name =
  window.prompt("Enter your name!", "<Your name>");
if (name != null) {
  window.alert("Hello, " + name + "!");
}
</script>
```

Prompting for User Data (prompt.html)

Figure 2.2   The input box generated
by window.prompt().

NOTE: Do note that if the Cancel button is clicked or the Esc key is pressed, window.prompt() returns null. The preceding code checks that; if the OK button is pressed, the data entered is shown.

3

Images and Animations

In the early days of the Web, one of the first effects done with JavaScript was image manipulation. A classical example was hover images: Hover the mouse pointer over an image and its appearance changes.

Netscape introduced JavaScript access for images in browser version 3. At that time, Internet Explorer 3 for Windows was in beta, so it was too late for this capability. However, Internet Explorer 3 for Macintosh was released after the Windows version, giving the Microsoft engineers enough time to add JavaScript image access to IE Mac. Beginning with IE 4, the Microsoft browser can access images as well, as do all other relevant browsers.

This allows not only nice graphical effects but also more sophisticated applications such as image slide shows.

Creating Mouseover Buttons

```
<img src="inactive.gif"
  onmouseover="this.src='active.gif';"
  onmouseover="this.src='inactive.gif';" />
```

One of the oldest effects in the World Wide Web consists of graphics that change their appearance when the mouse moves (hovers) over them. This is also called a "hover effect" or a "hover button"/"hover graphic." The name, by the way, is also reflected in the nonstandard hover pseudo CSS class some browsers support.

To change a graphic, you have to access it and then change its src property. Browsers support several methods of accessing graphics. The following ones work consistently across modern browsers:

- Set the image's name attribute, and access it via document.images["name"].

- Set the image's name attribute, and access it via document.images.name (however, then some special characters like blanks or dashes are not possible in the name attribute).

- Access the image using its position on the page, via the document.images array: document.images[0] for the first image, document.images[1] for the second image, and so forth.

- Set the image's id attribute, and access it via document.getElementById("id").

The appropriate event for the mouse moving over the image is mouseover, and when mouseout occurs, you should reset the image to its original state. The preceding code does this and puts everything in the <img> element, but you could also use a generic custom

JavaScript function for doing so. The following code creates a function that expects the image's name and its URL in a function and then calls this using onmouseover/onmouseout:

```
<script language="JavaScript"
  type="text/javascript">
function changeImage(name, url) {
  if (document.images[name]) {
    document.images[name].src = url;
  }
}
</script>
<img
  name="myImage"
  src="inactive.gif"
  onmouseover="changeImage('myImage',
➥'active.gif');"
  onmouseout="changeImage('myImage',
➥'inactive.gif');" />
```

A Hover Button (hover.html)

Figure 3.1 shows two buttons; the mouse pointer is over the one on the right, demonstrating both states of the button.

WARNING: Older browsers (including Netscape 4.x) do not support onmouseover/onmouseout for anything other than links. In that case, you have to embed the image within an HTML link and use onmouseover/onmouseout in the <a> tag:

```
<a
  href="#"
  onmouseover="..." onmouseout="">
  <img src="..." />
</a>
```

Figure 3.1   The buttons change their appearance
when the mouse hovers over them.

Preloading Images

```
var i = new Image();
i.src = "";
```

Although the mouseover effect from the previous
phrase is easy to implement and nice to look at, it still
has a structural flaw: After the mouse pointer moves
over an image, the replacement graphic is loaded from
the server. This leads to a certain latency and a possible
negative user experience.

Therefore, it is desirable to preload these images after
the page itself has been loaded. With JavaScript, you
can instruct the browser to load the images. Then they
are in the browser's cache (unless caching is disabled in
the browser or the web server sends HTTP headers
forbidding local caching) and load instantly when the
hover effect is triggered.

To achieve this effect, you have to instantiate the
JavaScript Image object and set its src property.

This loads the image in the background, without even displaying it. You just have to make sure that the preloading is executed when the HTML page has been fully loaded, as the following listing shows:

```
<script language="JavaScript"
  type="text/javascript">
function preloadImage(url) {
  var i = new Image();
  i.src = url;
}
</script>
<body onload="preloadImage('active.gif');">
</body>
```

Preloading Images (preload.html)

If several images have to be preloaded at once (for instance, if the whole navigation uses a hover effect), a more generic function accepting an array with images can be used:

```
<script language="JavaScript"
  type="text/javascript">
function preloadImages(urls) {
  var img = new Array();
  for (var i=0; i<urls.length; i++) {
    img[img.length] = new Image();
    img[img.length - 1].src = urls[i];
  }
}

window.onload = function() {
  var img = new Array(
    "active.gif", "inactive.gif", "other.gif");
```

```
  preloadImages(img);
}
</script>
```

Preloading Multiple Images (preload-array.html)

TIP: With standard HTML, you can preload images, as well, without having to display them:

```
<div style="display:none;">
  <img src="active.gif" height="1" width="1" />
  <img src="inactive.gif" height="1" width="1" />
  <img src="other.gif" height="1" width="1" />
</div>
```

However, when you need these images only for JavaScript effects, you should only preload them using JavaScript. Otherwise, users without JavaScript would preload the files, as well—without seeing the visual (JavaScript) effects.

Animating Graphics

```
document.images["animation"].src = urls[pos];
window.setTimeout("animate(" + (pos + 1) + ");",
    500);
```

The GIF file format, originally from CompuServe, is the only graphics format that supports animation and is supported by all popular browsers. However, it also has some severe limitations, most annoyingly the 8-bit color palette that allows only 256 colors to be used. So PNG-24 is the way to go, but unfortunately this format does not have animation capabilities.

In this case, JavaScript is the way to go. Changing a graphic is possible as shown in the preceding phrases, and the only ingredient missing is the use of `setInterval()` or `setTimeout()`. The following code iterates through an array of images and moves to the next image after 500 milliseconds (half a second) have elapsed:

```
<script language="JavaScript"
  type="text/javascript">
var urls;

function animate(pos) {
  pos %= urls.length;
  document.images["animation"].src = urls[pos];
  window.setTimeout("animate(" + (pos + 1) + ");",
    500);
}

window.onload = function() {
  urls = new Array(
    "0.png", "1.png", "2.png", "3.png",
    "4.png", "5.png", "6.png");
  animate(0);
}
</script>
<img src="0.png" name="animation" />
```

Animating Through Images (animate.html)

The `animate()` function expects one parameter: the position of the next image to show. The list of images to iterate through is saved in a global variable, since `setTimeout()` cannot use local variables that are not available in the global scope.

With pos %= urls.length, the pointer to the image list is set to the beginning after the last image has been shown, effectively generating an infinite loop. If you want the animation to end after the last image, replace this line with the following code:

```
if (pos == urls.length) {
  return false;
}
```

Stretching Graphics

```
document.images["bar"].width += 5;
```

Sometimes it is not even necessary to create several graphics to build an animation. Sometimes just stretching an image can create a nifty effect. Usually, this does not fare too well on the Web, since only bitmap file formats are supported (except for Flash or SVG, which is not available across browsers in their default setup). Therefore, stretching a graphic instructs the browser to calculate additional image information. Usually, this is done by copying pixels.

In the case of a progress bar, a simple graphic can suffice. In a simple example, use a 1×1-pixel image. If it is used in the HTML page with a width of 20 pixels and a height of 10 pixels, you get a 20×10-pixel image. By animating the width of the image with JavaScript, you can get the impression of a moving progress bar.

The width and height of an image can be accessed from JavaScript using the width and height properties, both readable and writable. The following code moves the progress bar, using a simple 1×1-pixel graphic, black.gif.

```
<script language="JavaScript"
  type="text/javascript">
function progress() {
  if (document.images["bar"].width < 200) {
    document.images["bar"].width += 5;
    document.images["bar"].height = 5;
  } else {
    clearInterval(ID);
  }
}

var ID;
window.onload = function() {
  ID = setInterval("progress();", 500);
}
</script>
<img src="black.gif" name="bar" />
```

An Animated Progress Bar (progress.html)

Figure 3.2 shows the example in action: The 1×1 image has been stretched dynamically by JavaScript. The progress() function is called every 500 millisecond, thanks to the setInterval() call. After the progess bar has reached its maximum length (in this example, arbitrarily 200 pixels), the animation is stopped with clearInterval().

Figure 3.2 The graphic is animated so that it looks like a progress bar.

WARNING: If you do not explicitly set the height of the progress bar image, stretching its width also stretches the height, ruining the desired effect.

Visualizing the Page Loading State with a Progress Bar

```
if (document.images[i].complete) {
  loaded++;
}
```

Whether or not a page has been completely loaded cannot be determined by JavaScript alone, but at least it can be sufficiently estimated. The `complete` property of an image provides a Boolean value telling whether the image has been completely loaded. Also, an image supports the `load` event, so `onload` can be used to trigger code execution after the image has been loaded.

The following code iterates through all images on the page and counts how many of them have been completely loaded. This generates an estimated percentage of how much of the page has been fully loaded. (Of course, not included are applets and embedded media; also, the image file sizes are not taken into account.)

```
<script language="JavaScript"
  type="text/javascript">
function showprogress() {
  if (document.images.length == 0) {
    return false;
  }
  var loaded = 0;
  for (var i=0; i<document.images.length; i++) {
```

```
    if (document.images[i].complete) {
      loaded++;
    }
  }
  var percentage = Math.round(
    100 * loaded / document.images.length);
  document.getElementById("progress").innerHTML =
    percentage + "% loaded";
  if (percentage == 100) {
    window.clearInterval(ID);
  }
}

var ID = window.setInterval("showprogress();", 500);
</script>
<p name="progress">0% loaded</p>
```

The Loading Progress Bar (loadprogress.html)

In order to actually reproduce this effect, you have to embed images in your page that take quite long to load, either because they are really large or because the server is under a heavy load. The code downloads for this book include the PHP script gfx.php that relies on PHP's GD extension and creates a randomly colored image with a time delay of up to 15 seconds. Figure 3.3 shows the result when two out of three graphics have been loaded.

NOTE: Other interesting events for images are abort (when the loading of the image is aborted by the user) and error (when there is an error loading the image, for instance, when the file does not exist). They can be used with the onabort and onerror event handlers.

Figure 3.3   The third graphic is still loading.

Using Image Maps

JavaScript can also be used within client-side image maps, but only in relatively few scenarios:

- Every link in the image map can be a `javascript:` link, thus enabling the browser to call JavaScript when the user clicks on a hotspot in the map.

- Events like `mouseover`, `mouseout`, and `load` are also available within image maps for shapes defined in the `<map>` element.

- The image map associated with an image can be set via JavaScript, using the `useMap` property. However, usually there is only one image map suitable for one image.

4

CSS

In the early days of the World Wide Web, content was king, the layout rather irrelevant. Then, the Web started to commercialize, and web developers started abusing HTML, which somehow transformed from the markup language it became to an inadequate design tool. With CSS (Cascading Style Sheets), the situation became quite a bit better, since it allowed styling the contents of an HTML page—HTML was a markup language again, defining the content and the structure of a page, but not necessarily how it looked.

Using JavaScript, CSS effects can be applied on the fly. Most of the phrases in this chapter are very generic in nature so that you can apply these techniques to any CSS design challenges you may face. Some phrases, however, solve very specific problems.

Accessing CSS Styles

```
document.getElementById("para").style.fontWeight =
    "strong";
```

JavaScript can set any CSS commands and is "almost" using the name of the CSS command as the JavaScript property. However, there is a problem: Some characters, like the dash, are not allowed within a JavaScript property. But many CSS commands like, for instance, font-weight, do have dashes in them. Therefore, the JavaScript language uses a lowerCamelCase syntax: Every component starts with an uppercase letter, but not the very first one. So the CSS command font-weight can be set using the fontWeight property.

All CSS commands may be accessed using the style property of every styleable HTML element on the page. There are two common ways to access these elements:

- Using event handlers in the form of HTML attributes, and submitting a reference to the current element as the parameter: <p onmouseover= "handlerFunction(this);" />.

- Accessing the element using document. getElementById().

The following listing shows the latter approach. The <p> element is selected using document.getElementById(); then the font-weight CSS command is set:

```
<script language="JavaScript"
  type="text/javascript">
function makeBold() {
```

```
  document.getElementById("para").style.fontWeight =
    "bold";
  window.setTimeout("makeLighter();", 1000);
}

function makeLighter() {
  document.getElementById("para").style.fontWeight =
    "lighter";
  window.setTimeout("makeBold();", 1000);
}

window.onload = makeBold;
</script>
<p id="para">CSS and JavaScript</p>
```

Changing a CSS Command (style.html)

TIP: When a Mozilla browser is used, the JavaScript console also shows an error when an invalid value for the chosen style will be applied, as Figure 4.1 shows. This is extremely convenient when you're debugging.

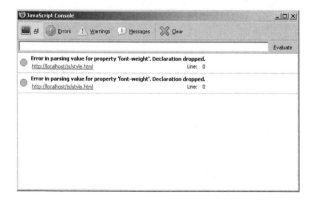

Figure 4.1   Mozilla browsers (here: Firefox) complain about invalid CSS values.

Accessing CSS Classes

```
document.getElementById("para").className =
  "strong";
```

The most commonly used way to apply CSS to an HTML page is by using classes. With JavaScript, the class for every element can be accessed with the className property. The following code implements the preceding phrase with the class approach:

```
<script language="JavaScript"
  type="text/javascript">
function makeBold() {
  document.getElementById("para").className =
    "strong";
  window.setTimeout("makeLighter();", 1000);
}

function makeLighter() {
  document.getElementById("para").className =
    "weak";
  window.setTimeout("makeBold();", 1000);
}

window.onload = makeBold;
</script>
<style type="text/css">
  .strong { font-weight: bold; }
  .weak { font-weight: lighter; }
</style>
<p id="para">CSS and JavaScript</p>
```

Changing the CSS Class (classname.html)

The preceding code changes the class for the text every second.

Accessing Individual Style Sheets

```
document.styleSheets[0].disabled = true;
```

When a page consists of more than one style sheet (<style> element with an inline style, or an external style sheet), you can use JavaScript to toggle between these style sheets, activate and deactivate them, and also combine them.

The styleSheets property of the document object contains all style sheets on the page, in the order in which they are loaded or appear on a page.

The most important property of every style sheet is disabled. If this is set to true, the style sheet becomes invisible and does not affect the layout of the page any longer.

There are two approaches to access a specific style sheet:

- Using the ID of the style sheet as the index for the styleSheets array.
- Using the number of the style sheet (starting at 0) as the index for the styleSheets array.

The former approach does not work well with Mozilla browsers, so you should use the numeric index, as the following code demonstrates:

```
<script language="JavaScript"
  type="text/javascript">
function makeBold() {
  document.styleSheets[0].disabled = false;
  document.styleSheets[1].disabled = true;
```

```
  window.setTimeout("makeLighter();", 1000);
}

function makeLighter() {
  document.styleSheets[0].disabled = true;
  document.styleSheets[1].disabled = false;
  window.setTimeout("makeBold();", 1000);
}

window.onload = makeBold;
</script>
<style type="text/css" id="strong">
  p { font-weight: bold; }
</style>
<style type="text/css" id="weak">
  p { font-weight: lighter; }
</style>
<p>CSS and JavaScript</p>
```

Changing the Style Sheet (stylesheets.html)

Accessing Individual CSS Rules

```
document.styleSheets[0].rules[0].style.color =
  randomColor();
document.styleSheets[0].cssRules[0].style.color =
  randomColor();
```

The individual rules within a style sheet can be pro-
grammatically accessed, as well. However, here, the web
browsers differ from each other. Internet Explorer supports the rules property, whereas all other browsers
use the cssRules property. The one exception is the
Opera browser, which supports neither of these two.

Note that you can access the rules and then, for instance, change them. Every rule behaves like a generic HTML element: You use the `style` property to access all styles, and then modify or add styles.

For the following example, a helper function generates a random color in RGB format:

```
function randomColor() {
  var chars = "0123456789abcdef";
  var color = "#";
  for (var i=0; i<6; i++) {
    var rnd = Math.floor(16 * Math.random());
    color += chars.charAt(rnd);
  }
  return color;
}
```

Then, the previous phrase is extended. First of all, every style sheet contains rules for both `<p>` and for `<span>` elements. Then, both of these rules get an additional CSS command: The color is set to a random value. You may question how useful this simple example is in the real world, but the technology behind it can be adapted in a quite flexible way.

```
<script language="JavaScript"
  type="text/javascript">
function makeBold() {
  document.styleSheets[0].disabled = false;
  document.styleSheets[1].disabled = true;
  if (document.styleSheets[0].rules) {
    document.styleSheets[0].rules[0].style.color =
      randomColor();
    document.styleSheets[0].rules[1].style.color =
      randomColor();
  } else if (document.styleSheets[0].cssRules) {
```

```
    document.styleSheets[0].cssRules[0].style.color =
      randomColor();
    document.styleSheets[0].cssRules[1].style.color =
      randomColor();
  }
  window.setTimeout("makeLighter();", 1000);
}

function makeLighter() {
  document.styleSheets[0].disabled = true;
  document.styleSheets[1].disabled = false;
  if (document.styleSheets[0].rules) {
    document.styleSheets[1].rules[0].style.color =
      randomColor();
    document.styleSheets[1].rules[1].style.color =
      randomColor();
  } else if (document.styleSheets[0].cssRules) {
    document.styleSheets[1].cssRules[0].style.color =
      randomColor();
    document.styleSheets[1].cssRules[1].style.color =
      randomColor();
  }
  window.setTimeout("makeBold();", 1000);
}

window.onload = makeBold;
</script>
<style type="text/css" id="strong">
  p { font-weight: bold; }
  span { font-style: italic; }
</style>
<style type="text/css" id="weak">
  p { font-weight: lighter; }
  span { font-style: normal; }
</style>
<p>CSS <span>and</span> JavaScript</p>
```

Accessing CSS Rules (rules.html)

Figure 4.2 shows the result: Even though the book is in grayscale, you can see the different colors (or: shades of gray) of the paragraph and the <span> element inside it.

Figure 4.2   The text colors are applied at random to the individual CSS rules.

Letting the Contents of a Website Disappear

```
document.getElementById(show).style.display =
    "block";
document.getElementById(hide).style.display =
    "none";
```

A quite common JavaScript effect on the web that uses CSS is to let elements of a page appear or disappear on request. Some pages implement a waiting screen on a slowly loading page; after the page has been loaded, the waiting screen disappears. Another example is to provide a number of tabs—only one is shown at a time, and switching between them is done using JavaScript, without the need of time-consuming requests to the server.

There are several ways to do this with JavaScript. You can use DOM, and you will find some phrases about letting DOM elements appear and disappear in Chapter 5, "DOM and DHTML." Two alternatives are presented in the phrase.

First, there is the visibility CSS command, which you can set to either visible or hidden to make the associated element appear or disappear. This translates to the JavaScript property visibility. Here is the code:

```
<script language="JavaScript"
  type="text/javascript">
  function showHide(show, hide) {
    document.getElementById(show).style.visibility =
      "visible";
    document.getElementById(hide).style.visibility =
      "hidden";
  }
</script>
<p> <br /> </p>
<p id="tab1"
  style="position: absolute; top: 5px; left: 5px;">
  Tab 1
</p>
<p id="tab2" style="position: absolute; top: 5px;
    left: 5px; visibility: hidden;">
  Tab 2
</p>
<input type="button" value="Tab 1"
  onclick="showHide('tab1', 'tab2');" />
<input type="button" value="Tab 2"
  onclick="showHide('tab2', 'tab1');" />
```

Setting the Visibility of an Element (visibility.html)

However, as you will see, the absolute positioning leads
to some subtle differences across browsers. The best
way is to use a block layout and set the display property of the element to either block or none:

```
<script language="JavaScript"
  type="text/javascript">
  function showHide(show, hide) {
    document.getElementById(show).style.display =
      "block";
    document.getElementById(hide).style.display =
      "none";
  }
</script>
<p id="tab1">
  Tab 1
</p>
<p id="tab2" style="display: none;">
  Tab 2
</p>
<input type="button" value="Tab 1"
  onclick="showHide('tab1', 'tab2');" />
<input type="button" value="Tab 2"
  onclick="showHide('tab2', 'tab1');" />
```

Setting the Display Mode of an Element (display.html)

Figure 4.3 shows the result: Clicking on the second
button shows the second tab.

Figure 4.3   Clicking on a button shows
the associated tab.

Applying JavaScript to CSS Selectors

```
Behaviour.register(cssrules);
```

In 1999, the W3C proposed "Behavioral Extensions to
CSS (http://w3.org/TR/1999/WD-becss-19990804),
an approach to bind JavaScript code to CSS behaviors.
The basic idea was to avoid use of the well-known
on*xxx* HTML attributes. After 1999, not much progress
was made in this area, but Ben Nolan managed to provide a workaround (read: hack) to allow a similar concept. For it to work, you need the JavaScript library
from http://www.bennolan.com/behaviour/, in form
of the file behaviour.js. (Note the British English
spelling of the word—a perfect addition to the phrasebook!) This code collection allows providing rules
containing JavaScript code in the form of CSS
selectors.

For it to work, you first need an external JavaScript file
that defines CSS rules. You basically create an object
with CSS selectors as the keys, and JavaScript event-
handling functions as the values. Then, you call the

`Behaviour.register()` method to report these rules to
the behaviour library:

```javascript
var cssrules = {
  "p.para" : function(e){
    e.onmouseover = function(){
      this.style.fontWeight = "bold";
    }
    e.onmouseout = function(){
      this.style.fontWeight = "normal";
    }
  },
  "#term" : function(e){
    e.onmouseover = function(){
      this.style.fontStyle = "oblique";
    },
    e.onmouseout = function(){
      this.style.fontStyle = "normal";
    }
  }
};

Behaviour.register(cssrules);
```

The CSS/JavaScript Rules (rules.js)

All that is left to do is to load both the JavaScript
library and the preceding rules JavaScript file. Then the
JavaScript code is executed when the associated events
(in the example: mouseover and mouseout) are fired.

```html
<script language="JavaScript"
  type="text/javascript" src="behaviour.js">
</script>
<script language="JavaScript"
  type="text/javascript" src="rules.js">
```

```
</script>
<p class="para">CSS <span id="term">and</span>
  JavaScript</p>
```

Using the Behaviour JavaScript Library (behaviour.html)

Figure 4.4 shows the result: When the mouse pointer is moved over the <span> element, two event handlers are called.

Figure 4.4   The JavaScript code gets executed.

NOTE: The main advantage of this approach lies in the fact that the JavaScript code completely resides in external files and is not cluttering the HTML markup of the page. From an architectural point of view, this is quite a bright idea—and it works cross-browser.

Changing the Mouse Cursor

```
document.getElementById("button").style.cursor =
  "help";
```

Every operating system comes with a certain set of mouse cursors, and CSS supports a subset of them.

The appearance is a bit different between operating systems, but the general layout is quite similar.

The CSS command in question is cursor, and it is also available from JavaScript, as the following code shows:

```
<script language="JavaScript"
  type="text/javascript">
window.onload = function() {
  document.getElementById("helpButton").style.cursor
➥= "help";
};
</script>
<input type="submit" id="helpButton" value="Get
help" />
```

Changing the Cursor (cursor.html)

You can see the result in Figure 4.5: The mouse cursor now includes a question mark to make it more obvious that there is help waiting behind the button.

Figure 4.5   The mouse cursor changes.

WARNING: Every mouse cursor fulfills its purpose. So you should really think twice before changing the appearance of the mouse cursor—do not irritate your users!

CSS Cursor Styles

These are the allowed values for the cursor
JavaScript/CSS property:

- auto
- crosshair
- default
- e-resize
- help
- move
- n-resize
- ne-resize

- nw-resize
- pointer
- s-resize
- se-resize
- sw-resize
- test
- w-resize
- wait

5

DOM and DHTML

This chapter covers two loosely related JavaScript techniques: DOM and DHTML. These two aspects of JavaScript have existed for several years, but only since the Netscape 4.x market share dropped under the Mozilla market share a few years ago has it been possible to use them together. Originally, they did not have much in common, but now they are often used together. The focus of this chapter is on DOM, since many of the phrases throughout this book can more or less be categorized under "DHTML."

Understanding DOM

DOM, which stands for Document Object Model, is quite self-describing: It provides an object model (and, alongside it, an API, or application programming interface) for a document. In the web context, this of course refers to an HTML document.

One of the best ways to visualize the DOM for a web page is to use the DOM Inspector that comes with Mozilla browsers. Within the Document Object

Model, all page elements are placed in a treelike hierarchy. Every HTML tag is a node within this tree, with subnodes and parent nodes. Also, every text portion is its own DOM node (a text node, to be exact). Figure 5.1 shows the DOM Inspector for a simple sample document.

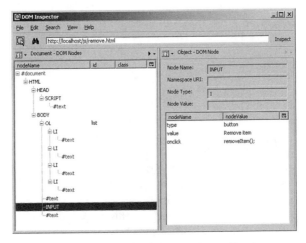

Figure 5.1 The DOM Inspector shows all nodes of a document.

Of course, the DOM API supports methods to not only access elements in the DOM tree, but also add and remove elements. Therefore, it is possible to modify virtually anything on the page.

One question remains: What is better, using the DOM or using some standard JavaScript objects like forms or images? Generally, the DOM way is much more flexible, but sometimes more difficult as well. Therefore, if there is a JavaScript shortcut you can use, go with it. Otherwise, familiarize yourself with the DOM.

NOTE: More DOM-related information can be found at the World Wide Web Consortium (W3C): http://w3c.org/DOM.

Understanding DHTML

Although DOM is a "real" technical term, DHTML—or Dynamic HTML—is not. DHTML is a pure marketing term. Back when the term was coined, all it meant was something along the lines of "JavaScript for browsers version number 4 and up." Back then, Netscape Navigator and Internet Explorer were fighting the legendary browser war, and with their version 4, both vendors included more dynamic JavaScript features, unfortunately quite incompatible with each other. Most DHTML effects now and then cover positioning elements and changing them upon user action.

With Netscape 4 and Internet Explorer 4 long gone, recent versions of both browser brands (remember that Netscape 6 followed Netscape 4 and is based on Mozilla's Gecko Engine) support DOM reasonably well (although there are still some missing elements). Therefore, DHTML was reborn, since dynamic JavaScript effects are nowadays possible with only a small amount of browser-specific code and client sniffing.

Accessing Specific Elements

```
document.getElementById("para")
```

When you're working with the DOM, the ideal way to later access an element on the page is by giving it a unique identifier, or ID. Then, the DOM method document.getElementById() accesses the given element and enables you to go on from there: Modify the element, append subelements, or otherwise further navigate through the DOM tree.

In the following example, the <p> element is accessed. Depending on the browser type, the string representation of the element class is different. Whereas Internet Explorer just outputs [object], Mozilla browsers are more verbose and provide more information: [object HTMLParagraphElement].

```
<script language="JavaScript"
  type="text/javascript">
window.onload = function() {
  window.alert(document.getElementById("para"));
}
</script>
<p id="para">JavaScript Phrasebook</p>
```

Accessing an Element By ID (getelementbyid.html)

WARNING: The DOM is accessible only when the whole document has been loaded. That's the reason the DOM access code is executed only after the load event has been fired.

Accessing Tags

```
document.getElementsByTagName("p")
```

An alternative way to access elements on the current page is to access them through the tag names.

Whenever you have to work on a set of elements that are represented by the same HTML tags (for instance, all list items or all paragraphs—everything that is not represented by another property of the JavaScript document object), the method document. getElementsByTagName() can be used. You provide the tag name and get an array of all elements, which you can then process further.

The following code just accesses all `<p>` elements and counts them:

```
<script language="JavaScript"
  type="text/javascript">
window.onload = function() {
  window.alert(
    document.getElementsByTagName("p") +
    " (" + document.getElementsByTagName("p").length
    + " elements)");
}
</script>
<p>JavaScript Phrasebook</p>
<p>Sams Publishing</p>
```

Accessing Elements By Tag Name (getelementsbytagname.html)

The output of the preceding code is `[object HTMLCollection]` (2 elements); Internet Explorer once again gives less information, outputting `[object]` (2 elements).

Navigating the DOM Tree

After you are inside the DOM, you can navigate in the DOM structure, going both up and down, to the left and to the right. Here is a list of the most important properties every DOM node has:

- firstChild: first child node
- lastChild: last child node
- childNodes: all child nodes (as an array)
- parentNode: parent node
- nextSibling: next node on the same level ("to the right")
- previousSibling: previous node on the same level ("to the left")

Also, nodeName returns the name of the tag of the node (or #text for text nodes), whereas nodeValue returns the value of a node (useful with text nodes).

Determining Node Information

```
s += nodeName + ": " + nodeValue +
  " (" + nodeType + ")\n";
```

As already mentioned in the previous phrase, it is possible to gather information about a node, which is extremely useful when working on arbitrary DOM data.

Whereas nodeName gives information about the name of the node (tag name or #text for text nodes), nodeValue is useful only for text nodes and returns the actual text in the node. The third category of information comes from the nodeType property, which gives information regarding the kind of node. Table 5.1 contains a list of all possible values for nodeType.

Table 5.1   Node Types

Node Type	Description
1	Tag
2	Attribute
3	Text (includes whitespace)
8	HTML comment
9	Document
10	DTD
11	Fragment

The following code then analyzes a simple DOM structure and outputs information regarding all child nodes. Figure 5.2 shows the output in the browser.

```
<script language="JavaScript"
  type="text/javascript">
window.onload = function() {
  var s = "";
  with (document.getElementById("para")) {
    for (var i=0; i<childNodes.length; i++) {
      with (childNodes[i]) {
        s += nodeName + ": " + nodeValue +
            " (" + nodeType + ")\n";
      }
    }
  }
  window.alert(s);
}
</script>
<p id="para"><em>JavaScript</em> Phrasebook</p>
```

Retrieving Node Information (nodeinfo.html)

Figure 5.2   Information about all child nodes.

Removing Elements

```
list.removeChild(list.lastChild);
```

The removeChild() method that every node has can be used to eliminate a node from the DOM tree. Note that you have to call this method from the parent element of the node to delete, and to provide the node as a parameter. The following sample shows a list and removes the last item every time the button is clicked; see Figure 5.3 for the output in the browser.

```
<script language="JavaScript"
  type="text/javascript">
function removeItem() {
  var list = document.getElementById("list");
  if (list.childNodes.length > 0) {
    list.removeChild(list.lastChild);
  }
}
</script>
<ol id="list">
  <li>Item</li>
```

```
   <li>Item</li>
   <li>Item</li>
   <li>Item</li>
</ol>
<input type="button" onclick="removeItem();"
  value="Remove item" />
```

Removing Nodes (remove.html)

Figure 5.3   The last node gets removed.

TIP: When you only have direct access to the node to delete (curNode in the following code), this approach will work:

`curNode.parentNode.removeChild(curNode);`

When you call this code in a handler function for the node itself, you can replace curNode with this.

Adding Elements

`list.appendChild(newNode);`

Creating new DOM nodes is done by the document.
createElement() method. It creates a new element,

using the tag name provided as a parameter. This element can then be inserted into the DOM tree. The (node) method that is used most of the time is appendChild(). It appends a new child to the end of the children list.

The following code adds a new, empty list element (<li>) to the end of the <ul> list whenever the button is clicked:

```
<script language="JavaScript"
  type="text/javascript">
function addItem() {
  var list = document.getElementById("list");
  var newNode = document.createElement("li");
  list.appendChild(newNode);
}
</script>
<ul id="list"><li>Item</li></ul>
<input type="button" onclick="addItem();"
  value="Add item" />
```

Adding Nodes (add.html)

The disadvantage of this approach is that the new element is always appended to the end of the children list. To mitigate this effect, the insertBefore() method allows inserting a new node *before* any other node (so you can insert it anywhere but at the end of the list—you still have appendChild() for this). As in parameters, you provide the new node first, then the new sibling.

The following code inserts a new <li> element to the *beginning* of the list anytime the button is clicked. This is documented in Figure 5.4.

```
<script language="JavaScript"
  type="text/javascript">
function addItem() {
  var list = document.getElementById("list");
  var newNode = document.createElement("li");
  list.insertBefore(newNode, list.firstChild);
}
</script>
<ul id="list"><li>Item</li></ul>
<input type="button" onclick=vaddItem();"
  value="Add item" />
```

Adding Nodes at the Beginning of the Children List (addbefore.html)

Figure 5.4 List elements are added to the
beginning of the list.

Creating Text Elements

```
var newTextNode =
  document.createTextNode("Item " + nr);
```

If you want to put text within an element, you need a
text node that is a subnode of the actual element node.
The createTextNode() method creates such a text
node; you just provide the actual text.

In the following code, once again list elements are added; however, this time they do get text inside them. So first you create a text node, and then you append this text node to another node (which then could be appended to another node, which could be appended to yet another node, which…you get the picture).

```
<script language="JavaScript"
  type="text/javascript">
var nr = 1;
function addItem() {
  var list = document.getElementById("list");
  var newNode = document.createElement("li");
  nr++;
  var newTextNode =
    document.createTextNode("Item " + nr);
  newNode.appendChild(newTextNode);
  list.appendChild(newNode);
}
</script>
<ul id="list"><li>Item 1</li></ul>
<input type="button" onclick="addItem();"
  value="Add item" />
```

Creating (and Adding) a Text Node (textnode.html)

Working with Attributes

```
newLink.setAttribute(
  "href", "http://www.samspublishing.com/");
```

So far, this chapter's phrases have covered both regular tags and text nodes. The one major thing still missing

is attributes. You can access attributes in the form of
nodes, but the most convenient way is to use the
setAttribute() method: Just provide the attribute
name and its value. In the following code, the contents
of the new <li> items are a hyperlink, with an href
attribute set:

```
<script language="JavaScript"
  type="text/javascript">
var nr = 1;
function addItem() {
  var list = document.getElementById("list");
  var newNode = document.createElement("li");
  var newLink = document.createElement("a");
  newLink.setAttribute("href",
    "http://www.samspublishing.com/");
  nr++;
  var newTextNode =
    document.createTextNode("Item " + nr);
  newLink.appendChild(newTextNode);
  newNode.appendChild(newLink);
  list.appendChild(newNode);
}
</script>
<ul id="list"><li>Item 1</li></ul>
<input type="button" onclick="addItem();"
  value="Add item" />
```

Setting Attributes (attributes.html)

Figure 5.5 shows that all links added to the list do
point to the provided URL.

Figure 5.5 Dynamically generated hyperlinks.

Cloning Elements

```
var newItem = oldItem.cloneNode(true);
```

Instead of creating new nodes all over again, you can also clone an existing node. The cloneNode() method that every node has does this for you. You can decide whether to clone only the node and its attribute, or to clone all child nodes (and their child nodes and so on) as well. If you provide true as the parameter for cloneNode(), a so-called "deep copy" also copies children; false copies only the node itself.

```
<script language="JavaScript"
  type="text/javascript">
var nr = 1;
function addItem(cloneMode) {
  var list = document.getElementById("list");
  var oldItem = list.firstChild;
  var newItem = oldItem.cloneNode(cloneMode);
  list.appendChild(newItem);
}
</script>
```

```
<ul id="list"><li><a href="http://www.
samspublishing.com/">Item 1</a></li></ul>
<input type="button" onclick="addItem(true);"
  value="Clone all" />
<input type="button" onclick="addItem(false);"
  value="Clone node only" />
```

Cloning Nodes (clone.html)

When you click on the first button, the whole node
(including subelements like the link and list item text)
are copied; the second button clones only the node
itself, generating a new but empty list item. Take a
look at Figure 5.6 to see the difference.

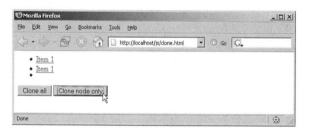

Figure 5.6   Two ways to copy nodes.

Replacing Elements

```
list.replaceChild(newNode, list.firstChild);
```

If you remove a node and then insert another one at
the same place, the replaceChild() method saves you a
bit of coding. You provide the new and the old node,
and JavaScript does the rest for you. Remember that

you have to call this method from the parent element of the old and the new node!

```
<script language="JavaScript"
  type="text/javascript">
var nr = 1;
function addItem() {
  var list = document.getElementById("list");
  var newNode = document.createElement("li");
  nr++;
  var newTextNode =
    document.createTextNode("Item " + nr);
  newNode.appendChild(newTextNode);
  list.replaceChild(newNode, list.firstChild);
}
</script>
<ul id="list"><li>Item 1</li></ul>
<input type="button" onclick="addItem();"
  value="Replace item" />
```

Replacing Nodes (replace.html)

The preceding code replaces the first child (node) of the list with a new node.

Creating a Bulleted List from JavaScript Data

```
var newItem = document.createElement("li");
var newText = document.createTextNode(data[i]);
newItem.appendChild(newText);
list.appendChild(newItem);
```

Especially in the context with Web Services and AJAX (see Chapters 10 and 11), you often receive data from

the server and have to display it in a dynamic way.
One good approach is to use an HTML list. The following code provides a function createList() that
expects an array with values and converts this into
a list.

```
<script language="JavaScript"
  type="text/javascript">
function createList(data) {
  var list = document.createElement("ul");
  for (var i = 0; i < data.length; i++) {
    var newItem = document.createElement("li");
    var newText = document.createTextNode(data[i]);
    newItem.appendChild(newText);
    list.appendChild(newItem);
  }
  return list;
}

window.onload = function() {
  var list = createList(
    ["one", "two", "three", "four", "five"]);
  document.body.appendChild(list);
}
</script>
```

Creating a List (list.html)

Note that document.body is a shortcut to the <body>
element (otherwise, you could use document.
getElementxByTagName("body")[0]); then appendChild()
adds the HTML list to the end of the page.

Creating a Table from JavaScript Data

```javascript
var td = document.createElement("td");
var newText = document.createTextNode(data[i][j]);
td.appendChild(newText);
tr.appendChild(td);
```

A bit more complicated than a list is a whole table. First, you have to use the <tbody> element (and may want to use <tbody> and/or <tfoot>, as well). Otherwise, you may not see anything in Internet Explorer.

The helper function createTable() expects a multi-dimensional array. Every array element itself is a list of values to be displayed in the table; the first array element contains the header text for each column.

As you can see, the code gets longer, but on the other hand the basic approach is the same: Create nodes and text nodes and then append them to each other in the correct order. Figure 5.7 shows the resulting table.

```html
<script language="JavaScript"
  type="text/javascript">
function createTable(data) {
  var table = document.createElement("table");
  var thead = document.createElement("thead");
  var tr = document.createElement("tr");
  for (var i = 0; i < data[0].length; i++) {
    var th = document.createElement("th");
    var newText =
      document.createTextNode(data[0][i]);
    th.appendChild(newText);
```

```
      tr.appendChild(th);
    }
    thead.appendChild(tr);
    table.appendChild(thead);

    var tbody = document.createElement("tbody");
    for (var i = 1; i < data.length; i++) {
      var tr = document.createElement("tr");
      for (var j=0; j < data[i].length; j++) {
        var td = document.createElement("td");
        var newText =
          document.createTextNode(data[i][j]);
        td.appendChild(newText);
        tr.appendChild(td);
      }
      tbody.appendChild(tr);
    }

    table.appendChild(tbody);
    return table;
}

window.onload = function() {
  var table = createTable([
    ["1", "2", "3", "4", "5"],
    ["one", "two", "three", "four", "five"],
    ["un", "deux", "trois", "quatre", "cinq"],
    ["eins", "zwei", "drei", "vier", "fünf"]]);
  document.body.appendChild(table);
}
</script>
```

Creating a Table (table.html)

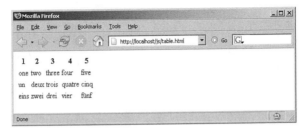

Figure 5.7   The dynamically generated table.

Changing HTML Fragments

`list.innerHTML += newNode;`

Changing text nodes (either by replacing them or by using the nodeValue property) changes only actual text, but you cannot change complete HTML fragments, including subelements. To do that, the innerHTML property of every element may prove useful. Although innerHTML is not standardized and is not part of any DOM specification, it works just fine. With innerHTML, you can change the inner HTML of any HTML element and even provide new subelements, as the following listing shows:

```
<script language="JavaScript"
  type="text/javascript">
var nr = 1;
function addItem() {
  var list = document.getElementById("list");
  nr++;
  var newNode = "<li>Item " + nr + "</li>";
  list.innerHTML += newNode;
}
```

```
</script>
<ul id="list"><li>Item 1</li></ul>
<input type="button" onclick="addItem();"
  value="Add item" />
```

Adding Elements via innerHTML (innerhtml.html)

So instead of using the clean and inconvenient DOM approach, innerHTML just writes the HTML into one element. Both approaches have their individual advantages and disadvantages: innerHTML requires that you take care of character encoding by yourself, but on the other hand it allows you to add or change several elements at once.

Positioning Elements

```
el.style.left = "0px";
el.style.posLeft = 0;
el.style.top = "0px";
el.style.posTop = 0;
```

CSS supports two ways to position an element: absolute positioning and relative positioning. No matter which method you choose, with JavaScript you can set the positioning values. Usually, the absolute positioning is more convenient since you do not have to calculate relative positions of nested elements then.

In most browsers, the left property defines the x coordinate of the element, and the top property is used for the y coordinate. The values are not numeric but—as usual in CSS—include a unit, usually px for pixels.

For Internet Explorer, you need a different approach. The posLeft and posTop properties set the horizontal and vertical position; however, this time, you just provide a numeric value, no unit.

The most convenient approach is to just set all of these properties, since there are no side effects. This saves you from client sniffing.

The following code positions the `<div>` element in the upper-left corner. Note that this element now lies over the text on the page.

```
<script language="JavaScript"
  type="text/javascript">
function position() {
  var el = document.getElementById("element");
  el.style.left = "0px";
  el.style.posLeft = 0;
  el.style.top = "0px";
  el.style.posTop = 0;
}
window.onload = position;
</script>
<h1>My Portal</h1>
<p>Some sample text. Some sample text.
  Some sample text. Some sample text.
  Some sample text. Some sample text.
  Some sample text. Some sample text.
  Some sample text. Some sample text.
  Some sample text. Some sample text. </p>
<div id="element" style="position: absolute;
background-color: #eee; border: 1px solid">
JavaScript Phrasebook
</div>
```

Positioning an Element (position.html)

Moving Elements

```
id = window.setInterval("animate();", 100);
```

A rather rare, but still used, DHTML scenario is not only positioning an element, but also moving and therefore animating an element. To do so, `window.setTimeout()` and `window.setInterval()` come in handy. The following code animates an ad banner diagonally over the page. The only potential issue is how to animate the position. For the Internet Explorer properties (`posLeft`, `posTop`), just adding a value suffices. For `left` and `top`, you first have to determine the old position and then add a value to it. The JavaScript function `parseInt()` extracts the numeric content from a string like `"123px"`. However, `parseInt()` returns `NaN` if no value is found in `left` or `top`. Therefore, the following helper function takes care of this situation; in this case, 0 is returned instead:

```
function myParseInt(s) {
  var ret = parseInt(s);
  return (isNaN(ret) ? 0 : ret);
}
```

Then, the following code animates the banner and stops after 50 iterations:

```
<script language="JavaScript"
  type="text/javascript">
var nr = 0;
var id = null;
function animate() {
  nr++;
  if (nr > 50) {
    window.clearInterval(id);
```

```
      document.getElementById("element").style
➥.visibility = "hidden";
  } else {
    var el = document.getElementById("element");
    el.style.left =
      (myParseInt(el.style.left) + 5) + "px";
    el.style.posLeft += 5;
    el.style.top =
      (myParseInt(el.style.top) + 5) + "px";
    el.style.posTop += 5;
  }
}
window.onload = function() {
  id = window.setInterval("animate();", 100);
};
</script>
<h1>My Portal</h1>
<div id="element" style="position: absolute;
background-color: #eee; border: 1px solid">
JavaScript Phrasebook
</div>
```

Animating an Element (animate.html; excerpt)

Creating a Sticky Navigation

```
window.onload = positionNavigation;
window.onscroll = positionNavigation;
```

Sometimes it is important that one part of a page is
always visible. Depending on the nature of the site, this
can be an ad banner (Geocities, now a part of Yahoo!,
was among the first to implement this) or a navigation.
Once again, a <div> element will be positioned. The
special feature of a sticky navigation is that the position

stays the same even if the user is scrolling. So the preceding code is used to call the positioning code both
when the page loads and when it scrolls.

For calculating the new position, you have to calculate
the current scroll offset. Internet Explorer provides
`document.body.scrollLeft` and `document.body.scrollTop`
for that; the other browsers use `window.pageXOffset` and
`window.pageYOffset`. The following code maintains
the position of the navigation, and Figure 5.8 shows
the result.

```
<script language="JavaScript"
  type="text/javascript">
function positionNavigation() {
  var nav = document.getElementById("navigation");
  var x, y;
  var navwidth = 155;
  if (window.innerWidth) {
    x = window.innerWidth + window.pageXOffset -
        navwidth;
    y = window.pageYOffset + 10;
  } else {
    with (document.body) {
      x = clientWidth + scrollLeft - navwidth;
      y = scrollTop + 10;
    }
  }
  nav.style.left = x + "px";
  nav.style.posLeft = x;
  nav.style.top = y + "px";
  nav.style.posTop = y;
}
window.onload = positionNavigation;
window.onscroll = positionNavigation;
</script>
<h1>My Portal</h1>
```

```
<div id="navigation" style="position: absolute;
background-color: #eee; border: 1px solid">
<a href="http://www.samspublishing.com/">Sams
Publishing</a><br />
<a href="http://www.amazon.com/gp/product/
0672328801">This book at Amazon</a><br />
<a href="http://www.hauser-wenz.de/blog/">Author's
weblog</a>
</div>
```

Maintaining the Position of an Element (sticky.html; excerpt)

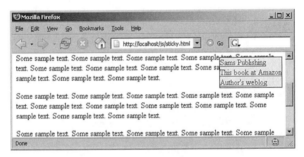

Figure 5.8   A sticky navigation with JavaScript.

Creating a Flash Pop-Up Ad

```
<param name="wmode" value="transparent" />
```

With pop-up blockers becoming more and more common in web browsers, creators of web advertisements have to become more creative. One way is to use a neglected feature of Flash movies embedded in the page: When you set the wmode parameter to "transparent" as shown in the preceding code, the Flash movie is

transparent, so you can place it over the content of the
page, creating a pop-up.

The file `flashad.swf` is a simple Flash animation that
includes a button that makes the ad disappear when
the user clicks on it. The following ActionScript code
(a language also based on ECMAScript) does this by
calling JavaScript code in the browser:

```
on (release) {
  getURL("javascript:void(document.getElementById(
➥'banner').style.visibility='hidden');");
}
```

The code of the page itself is quite similar to the code
from the previous phrase: Just as in a sticky navigation,
the Flash ad should always be visible.

```
if (window.innerWidth) {
  x = window.pageXOffset +
    Math.round((window.innerWidth - navwidth) / 2);
  y = window.pageYOffset + 10;
} else {
  with (document.body) {
    x = scrollLeft +
      Math.round((clientWidth - navwidth) / 2);
    y = scrollTop + 10;
  }
}
```

*A Transparent Flash Ad Banner, JavaScript Section (flashad.html;
excerpt)*

The banner itself resides in a `<div>` element. Take care
that the ID of the banner corresponds to the ID the
ActionScript code is trying to make invisible.

```
<div id="banner" style="position: absolute;">
<object
classid="clsid:d27cdb6e-ae6d-11cf-96b8-444553540000"
  codebase="http://fpdownload.macromedia.com/pub/
  shockwave/cabs/flash/swflash.cab#version=7,0,0,0"
  width="400" height="550" id="flashad">
  <param name="movie" value="flashad.swf" />
  <param name="quality" value="high" />
  <param name="wmode" value="transparent" />
  <param name="bgcolor" value="#ffffff" />
  <embed src="flashad.swf" quality="high"
      wmode="transparent" bgcolor="#ffffff"
      width="400" height="550" name="flashad"
      type="application/x-shockwave-flash"
      pluginspage="http://www.macromedia.com/go/
      getflashplayer" />
</object>
</div>
```

A Transparent Flash Ad Banner, HTML Section (flashad.html; excerpt)

Figure 5.9 shows the result: The banner resides over the content of the page; also, the background of the Flash movie is transparent.

Figure 5.9   A transparent flash banner.

WARNING: Just because Flash ads do not use pop-up windows does not mean that users hate them any less than pop-ups. So use this technique wisely, and make sure that users can actually make the ad invisible. Otherwise, the page content is not visible—and the user and potential customer will become invisible, as well.

OOP and Events

The more advanced JavaScript applications get, the greater is the need for structuring the code well. One way to do so is by using OOP, object-oriented programming. JavaScript itself is not an object-oriented language, but rather an object-based language. So there is a support for OOP, though it's somewhat limited.

The second topic of this chapter is the general JavaScript event handling. Apart from the basics, special events (mouse and keyboard) are covered.

Creating a Class

```
function UniversalClass() { }
```

There is no distinctive keyword for classes in JavaScript. Instead, each class is defined as a function. The difference between a regular function and this one is the way this function is later called: with the new keyword. The following listing implements a simple class; upon instantiation, the window.alert() box pops up.

```
<script language="JavaScript"
  type="text/javascript">
function UniversalClass() {
  window.alert("Welcome to my class!");
}

var uc = new UniversalClass();
</script>
```

A Simple Class (class.html)

Accessing Class Members

```
this.Count = count;
```

When you're working with class members, the most important aspect is to explicitly define all members. To allow external code to access the class members (properties and methods), the `this` keyword must be used. So if you define a function XYZ() within the class, it is available as a class method only if you add this code:

```
this.XYZ = XYZ;
```

Within this method, you can also access class properties using `this`; however, they have to be defined as well. For accessing class members both internally and externally, the dot (.) is used to separate instance name and member name.

The following code implements a simple class. The only class method, Count() (internal name: count()), takes one parameter and then counts in the given language. Figure 6.1 shows the result.

```
<script language="JavaScript"
  type="text/javascript">
function UniversalCounter() {
  this.copyright = "(C) 2006 JavaScript Phrasebook";
  this.Count = count;
  var numbers = {
    "en": "one, two, three",
    "fr": "un, deux, trois",
    "de": "eins, zwei, drei"
  };
  function count(language) {
    if (numbers[language]) {
      window.alert(numbers[language]);
    } else {
      window.alert("Unknown language");
    }
  }
}

var uc = new UniversalCounter();
uc.Count("fr");
</script>
```

A Class with Members (members.html)

Figure 6.1   The "Universal Counter."

NOTE: Another way to create objects is to use the Object constructor, in the following fashion:

```
var uc = new Object();
uc.copyright = "(C) 2006 JavaScript Phrasebook ";
uc.printCopyright = function() {
  window.alert(this.copyright);
};
```

Emulating Private Class Members

JavaScript does not have class modifiers like public, protected, and private that define who may access class members and who may not. However, as you can see in the previous phrase, there is quite an easy way to emulate private class members: If you do not "register" a variable or function within the class using the this keyword, it is visible only internally. In the previous phrase, the numbers object cannot be accessed from the outside, but is used internally by the Count()/count() method.

Inheriting Classes

```
UniversalCounter.prototype =
  new UniversalTranslator();
```

JavaScript does not enjoy an inheritance system for classes. However, via use of the prototype keyword, something similar can be—once again—emulated. With prototype, you can provide class members that are valid for all objects, including inherited ones. When JavaScript has to look up a property or method (for

example, when object.methodname() will be executed),
JavaScript first looks into the class and then looks
into the prototype object. This allows some kind of
inheritance.

In the following example, the UniversalTranslator
class defines a member (copyright). Then, the
UniversalCounter() class is implemented in a similar
fashion as before. The following command sets the
prototype property of the UniversalCounter class to a
new instance of the UniversalTranslator class.
Consequence: The UniversalCounter class inherits all
properties of the UniversalTranslator class and can
access it:

```
<script language="JavaScript"
  type="text/javascript">
function UniversalTranslator() {
  this.copyright = "(C) 2006 JavaScript Phrasebook";
}

function UniversalCounter() {
  this.Count = count;

  var numbers = {
    "en": "one, two, three",
    "fr": "un, deux, trois",
    "de": "eins, zwei, drei"
  };
  function count(language) {
    if (numbers[language]) {
      window.alert(numbers[language] +
        " [" + this.copyright + "]");
    } else {
      window.alert("Unknown language");
    }
  }
}
```

```
}
UniversalCounter.prototype =
  new UniversalTranslator();

var uc = new UniversalCounter();
uc.Count("de");
</script>
```

Class Inheritance with Prototype (inheritance.html)

Figure 6.2 shows that this really works: The copyright property can be accessed from the UniversalCounter class although it is defined in the UniversalTranslator class.

Figure 6.2 The inherited class property is shown.

WARNING: Only class members are inherited, but not class constructor code. If you want to do this as well, you have to define a specific method to be the class constructor, and call it manually in the derived class.

Extending Built-In JavaScript Objects

```
Date.prototype.isLeapYear = isLeapYear;
```

The prototype property can also be used to extend built-in JavaScript classes. In the following code, a function, isLeapYear(), is implemented that determines whether the return value of getFullYear() is a leap year. Note that the getFullYear() method is not implemented; using the prototype property, however, isLeapYear() becomes a method of the Date object and thus also has access to Date.getFullYear().

```
<script language="JavaScript"
  type="text/javascript">
function isLeapYear() {
  var y = this.getFullYear();
  return (y % 4 == 0 &&
          (y % 100 != 0 || y % 400 == 0));
}
Date.prototype.isLeapYear = isLeapYear;

var d = new Date();
window.alert(d.isLeapYear());
</script>
```

Extending the Date Class (extend.html)

JavaScript OOP Enhancements in Microsoft Atlas

The Microsoft AJAX Framework Atlas (http://atlas.asp.net/) also implements several new OOP extensions to JavaScript, making some standard OOP techniques simpler to implement. Among these features are the following:

- Namespaces
- Inheritance and access to base methods
- Abstract classes and methods
- Interfaces

Especially with the new AJAX hype, more and more libraries emerge that also spice up JavaScript's OOP support. Another option that demonstrates JavaScript OOP well is prototype.js (http://prototype.conio.net/).

Reacting Upon JavaScript Events

```
button.addEventListener("click", eventHandler,
    false);
button.attachEvent("onclick", eventHandler);
```

Reacting on JavaScript events can be done in different ways:

- Using an HTML attribute:
  ```
  <body onload="xyz();">
  ```

- Using the onXXX JavaScript attribute:
  ```
  window.onload = xyz;
  ```

However, there are various, competing event mechanisms in the different browsers. Internet Explorer supports attaching events to an element using the attachEvent() method. The name of the event here equals the HTML attribute, so you use "onload", for instance (though the event itself is called "load").

All other relevant browsers support the addEventListener() method, a part of the W3C model. Here, you provide the name of the event, so just "load" instead of "onload".

The following example shows how to attach an event to a button in a cross-browser fashion:

```
<script language="JavaScript"
  type="text/javascript">
function eventHandler() {
  window.alert("Event fired!");
}

window.onload = function() {
  var button =
    document.getElementById("eventButton");
  if (button.addEventListener) {
    button.addEventListener("click", eventHandler,
      false);
  } else if (button.attachEvent) {
    button.attachEvent("onclick", eventHandler);
  }
};
</script>
<input type="button" id="eventButton"
  value="Click me!" />
```

Attaching an Event (attach.html)

> **NOTE:** You can remove event handlers, as well. Internet Explorer uses detachEvent(), whereas other browsers follow the W3C and name their function removeEventListener().

Understanding Event Bubbling

When it comes to event handling, today's browsers support one of two concepts. Internet Explorer works with the so-called "event bubbling": An event is first fired from the very element where it occurs, and then bubbles up the DOM structure. Therefore, it is possible to capture and react upon this event at various places. For instance, imagine the following markup:

```
<div><p><em>JavaScript</em> Phrasebook</p></div>
```

If the mouse hovers over the text JavaScript, the mouseover event is first fired in the <em> element and then bubbles up to the <p> and <div> elements.

The competing model is the W3C model, which is supported by Mozilla browsers, Opera, and Safari/Konqueror. Here, the events are first sinking downward to the target element, and then bubbling up. So in the previous example, the event "visits" the <div>, <p>, and <em> elements and then bubbles up again via the <p> and <div> elements. When adding an event listener, you can specify in the third parameter of addEventListener() whether the event will be intercepted during sinking down (true) or bubbling up (false).

After an event has been intercepted, it is also possible to stop it from sinking down or bubbling up.

In Internet Explorer, set the event's `cancelBubble` property to `false`:

```
window.event.cancelBubble = false;
```

The W3C model supports the `stopPropagation()` method:

```
e.stopPropagation();
```

As you can see, in Internet Explorer the current event is always available via `window.event`, whereas other browsers automatically receive the event as the parameter (here called `e`) for the event listener.

Using Keyboard Events

```
document.onkeydown = showKey;
```

Keyboard events are not part of DOM Level 1 or Level 2, but are still implemented in recent browsers. Accessing the events differs from the usual approach (`window.event` in Internet Explorer; the event as the automatic parameter of the function in all other browsers). But then, the `keyCode` property returns the ASCII code of the key, which can then be processed, as in the following code:

```
done. Christian<script language="JavaScript"
  type="text/javascript">
function showKey(e) {
  var key;
  if (window.event) {
    key = window.event.keyCode;
  } else {
    key = e.keyCode;
```

```
  }
  key = String.fromCharCode(key);
  document.getElementById("para").innerHTML += key;
}

window.onload = function() {
  document.onkeydown = showKey;
}
</script>
<p id="para">Click and type here: </p>
```

Listening to Keyboard Events (key.html)

Figure 6.3 shows the result. The keys that are pressed are shown.

Figure 6.3   The key pressed is shown.

NOTE: All characters in Figure 6.3 are shown in uppercase, since JavaScript always takes into consideration which key was pressed, not whether it was upper- or lowercase. You can, however, also find out whether special keys were pressed by taking a look at the altKey, ctrlKey, and shiftKey properties.

Submitting a Form with the Enter Key

```
if (key == 13) {
  document.forms[0].submit();
}
```

Depending on the browser type and configuration, pressing the Enter key while in a form field does not always submit the form. Sometimes, for instance, the button that submits the form resides in another frame. In that case, adding a bit of JavaScript to ensure that the Enter key sends the form data, as well, comes in handy.

All that is necessary to implement for that functionality is the standard key event listener from the previous phrase. The key code for the Enter key is 13, so when this code is found, the form is submitted:

```
<script language="JavaScript"
  type="text/javascript">
function checkKey(e) {
  var key;
  if (window.event) {
    key = window.event.keyCode;
  } else {
    key = e.keyCode;
  }
  if (key == 13) {
    document.forms[0].submit();
  }
}
window.onload = function() {
  document.forms[0].elements["field"].onkeydown =
checkKey;
```

```
}
</script>
<form>
<input name="field" type="text" />
</form>
```

*Submitting a Form When Enter Has Been Pressed
(formsubmit.html)*

Using Mouse Events

```
document.onmousemove = showPosition;
```

When the mouse is being used, there is one quite
interesting event to listen to (apart from click, of
course): mousemove. The mouse position can be determined by looking at certain properties. Again, these
properties depend on which of the two browser
groups the client belongs to: Internet Explorer or the
rest of the world:

- clientX and clientY for Internet Explorer
- pageX and pageY for all other browsers

Here is a complete listing that shows the current
mouse position in the status bar of the browser (if
available):

```
<script language="JavaScript"
  type="text/javascript">
function showPosition(e) {
  var x, y;
  if (window.event) {
```

```
    x = window.event.clientX;
    y = window.event.clientY;
  } else {
    x = e.pageX;
    y = e.pageY;
  }
  window.status = "x: " + x + ", y: " + y;
}
window.onload = function() {
  document.onmousemove = showPosition;
}
</script>
```

Tracking Mouse Movements (mouse.html)

WARNING: Some browsers do not allow JavaScript to update the status bar, for instance, recent Firefox versions. You do not get an error message, but the status bar remains unchanged. Figure 6.4 shows the result in a browser that does support changing the text in the status bar.

Figure 6.4   The mouse position is
continuously updated.

Distinguishing Mouse Buttons

When it comes to finding out which mouse button has been pressed (when you listen to the click event), the browsers once again have different solutions. Both solutions use the button property of the event property, but the values are different.

Mozilla follows the W3C standard: 0 means left button, 1 means middle button, 2 means right button. However, the rest of the world, which includes Microsoft and other browsers, supports a more logical way: 1 means left button, 2 means right button, and 4 means middle button. As you can see from these numbers, these are all powers of 2. Therefore, you can combine these values. For instance, a value of 3 means that both the left and the right button have been pressed at the same time.

7

Cookies

JavaScript is a purely client-side technology. Admittedly, it is possible to use JavaScript on the server, but this has nothing to do with JavaScript running in the browser; it is a similar syntax in a completely different context.

Usually, JavaScript is completely restricted to the current page and does not have access to something from the server. There are very few exceptions to this rule. One exception can be found in Chapter 11, "AJAX (and Related Topics)," and another one is covered in this chapter.

Cookies are not a specific browser technology, but a mechanism in the client/server model to overcome one major shortcoming in the HTTP protocol. HTTP is stateless, which means that the protocol does not have a memory. A client opens a connection to a server, retrieves a document (or an image or any other data), and then closes the connection. The next time data is sent to this specific client from the server, the server does not recognize the client.

Cookies can help work around this situation. A server can send a short bit of text information to the client, the so-called cookie. If—and only if—this data is accepted and locally saved, the client sends this data back with every request to the same server. This enables the server application to recognize the user again.

The good thing: JavaScript can both get (read) and set (write) cookies, avoiding the HTTP protocol. This allows some scenarios that are not possible with HTTP and a server-side technology alone.

Other mechanisms to achieve a similar result are sessions, but this is something that must be implemented by the server-side technology, unrelated to JavaScript.

Understanding Cookies

When a web server sends a cookie to a client, an HTTP header entry in the following fashion is used:

```
Set-Cookie: session=abcd1234; expires=Tue,
➡20-Feb-2007 12:10:52 GMT; path=/;
➡domain=.samspublishing.com
```

Then the client receives this cookie information and, according to the client capabilities and/or its configuration, takes one of the following four actions:

- The client ignores the cookie.
- The client accepts the cookie.
- The client asks the user whether to accept the cookie.
- The client rejects the cookie.

Actually, the first and the last actions are the same. It is not possible for the web server to find out whether a cookie has been refused by the user, refused by the client configuration, or ignored by the client due to a lack of cookie support.

If accepted, cookies are then sent back to the server if a combination of requirements is met. The associated HTTP header entry then looks like this:

```
Cookie: session=abcd1234
```

A cookie can be tied to a domain and a path. Therefore, a cookie is usually sent back only to the server it originated from. It is possible to overwrite the domain value in a cookie, but some browsers then automatically refuse this cookie.

Also, there are some limitations for cookies. Not all browsers support them in a similar fashion, but the following requirements are the minimum set a browser must support:

- 4KB (4096 bytes) per cookie
- 20 cookies per domain
- 300 cookies total

NOTE: There is no official cookie specification that is supported across browsers, but all relevant clients support a proprietary "preliminary" specification Netscape published in the 1990s. It is still available for viewing at http://wp.netscape.com/newsref/std/cookie_spec.html.

Setting Cookies

```
document.cookie = "myLanguage=JavaScript";
```

Setting a cookie with JavaScript equals setting the
cookie property of the document object. It is important
to use the same format the HTTP protocol uses for
sending a cookie to the client. For "regular cookies"
(cookies without expiration dates or other restrictions,
as detailed in the following phrases), the name and the
value of the cookie have to be separated by an equal
sign. The name of the cookie must not contain
any special characters like spaces, semicolons, and
whitespace; such special characters in the cookie value
should be URL-encoded (for instance, a space character turns into %20, the hexadecimal representation of its
ASCII value). The specification recommends the
encoding, but does not prescribe it.

As the following listing shows, setting more than one
cookie can be achieved by setting multiple values to
document.cookie. Therefore, writing to document.cookie
does not overwrite any previous cookies, but is just
adding cookies. The only exception to this rule: If a
cookie of the same name exists, the client tries to
overwrite it.

```
<script language="JavaScript"
  type="text/javascript">
document.cookie = "myLanguage=JavaScript";
document.cookie =
  "myOtherLanguage=PHP:%20Hypertext%20Preprocessor"
</script>
```

Setting a Cookie with JavaScript (setcookie.html)

Figure 7.1 shows the result in the browser if it's configured to ask the user before setting a cookie.

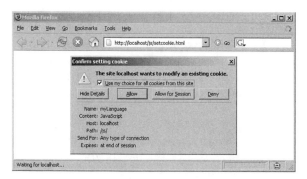

Figure 7.1   The browser tries to set the cookie sent from JavaScript.

Reading Out Cookies

```
var cookies = document.cookie.split(/; /g);
```

When accessing `document.cookie`, JavaScript retrieves a list of all cookies the browser would send to the current server. Unfortunately, this access is not available in the form of an array, but of a string. For instance, the previous phrase would generate the following value for `document.cookie`:

```
myLanguage=JavaScript;
➥myOtherLanguage=PHP:%20Hypertext%20Preprocessor
```

Therefore, to get cookies out of this value, the following steps must be taken:

1. Split the cookie string at "; " (to get individual cookies).

2. Identify the first equal sign (=) in every cookie as the name/value delimiter.

Since the cookie values may contain equal signs as well, the first occurrence of an equal sign must be used. The following code prints out all cookies in the form of an HTML table. Before it's written to the page, HTML special characters are properly escaped with an HtmlEscape() function.

```javascript
<script language="JavaScript"
  type="text/javascript">
document.write("<table><tr><th>Name</th>
    ➥<th>Value</th></tr>");
var cookies = document.cookie.split(/; /g);
for (var i=0; i<cookies.length; i++) {
  var cookie = cookies[i];
  if (cookie.indexOf("=") == -1) {
    continue;
  }
  var name =
    cookie.substring(0, cookie.indexOf("="));
  var value =
    cookie.substring(cookie.indexOf("=") + 1);
  document.write("<tr><td>" +
                  HtmlEscape(name) +
                  "</td><td>" +
                  HtmlEscape(unescape(value)) +
                  "</td></tr>");
}
document.write("</table>");
</script>
```

Reading Out Cookies (getcookies.html; excerpt)

Figure 7.2 shows the possible output of the preceding listing.

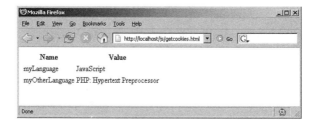

Figure 7.2   All cookies in the system are printed
in the browser.

When the value of one specific cookie is required, a
helper function may come in handy. It looks for the
given cookie name and returns the value (which is
everything to the right of the cookie name, until the
next semicolon or the end of the string):

```
function getCookie(name) {
  var pos = document.cookie.indexOf(name + "=");
  if (pos == -1) {
    return null;
  } else {
    var pos2 = document.cookie.indexOf(";", pos);
    if (pos2 == -1) {
      return unescape(
        document.cookie.substring(
          pos + name.length + 1));
    } else {
      return unescape(
        document.cookie.substring(
          pos + name.length + 1, pos2));
    }
  }
}
```

Reading Out a Single Cookie (getsinglecookie.html)

> **TIP:** Never forget to unescape the cookie value data. In the given example, this was done by using unescape() because the original cookies were escaped using escape(). If you are using another escaping scheme, you have to use the proper unescaping mechanism in your code.

Setting an Expiration Date

```
document.cookie="myLanguage=JavaScript; expires=
➥Tue, 25-Dec-2007 12:34:56 GMT"
```

By default, cookies expire when the user closes the browser. These cookies are then called temporary cookies. The opposite are persistent cookies, meaning cookies that live longer than the browser session. So when the browser is restarted, the cookie is still there.

For this to work, the cookie needs an expiration date detailing how long the cookie may remain in the browser. The cookie specification demands that the expiration date is provided in GMT (Greenwich mean time), and that the following format is used:

```
Wdy, DD-Mon-YYYY HH:MM:SS GMT
```

Here is a possible value:

```
Tue, 25-Dec-2007 12:34:56 GMT
```

This makes determining the correct date information (especially the weekday) quite hard; eventually, external libraries that can help with this task come in handy.

When the date is determined, it just has to be used in the value for document.cookie, as the code at the beginning of this phrase has demonstrated (see expirecookie.html).

Figure 7.3 shows the output of this code on a system that uses the GMT+1 time zone and therefore is one hour ahead of GMT. Of course, this information is displayed only when the browser is configured to ask the user when a cookie arrives.

Figure 7.3 This cookie comes with an expiration date.

Using Other Cookie Options

```
document.cookie="myLanguage=JavaScript; expires=
➥Tue, 25-Dec-2007 12:34:56 GMT; path=/;
➥domain=.example.com; secure"
```

Although the expiration date of a cookie is by far the most commonly used feature, there are others as well:

- path—This sets the path to tie the cookie to. The default value is the current path. If this is set to /, the whole website receives the cookie.

- domain—This specifies which domain(s) to use. By specification, at least two dots are required in the domain name, but many browsers ignore that.

If this is set to .example.com, then www.example.com and subdomain.example.com receive the cookie.

- secure—If this is set (just by putting it in the cookie string), the cookie is transmitted only via a secured connection (HTTPS).

The preceding code sets a cookie that is tied to the .example.com domain and will be transmitted via HTTPS connections only. Do note that the associated listing (cookieoptions.html) most probably will not work on your system unless you change the domain name to the actual domain name you are using.

WARNING: When you want to overwrite a cookie, make sure that you are using the same cookie features (name, path, domain, secure) as when you set the cookie; the expiration date and the cookie value may change, of course. Otherwise, the browser creates a new cookie.

Using HTTP Only Cookies

Recent versions of Microsoft's Internet Explorer web browser support an additional option for cookies: HttpOnly. If this is set, the cookie is transmitted via HTTP only but cannot be read out using JavaScript. This option has been introduced to avoid some security issues on some websites allowing the theft of sensible cookie data with JavaScript. However, HttpOnly is proprietary and is supported only in Microsoft browsers. More information on HttpOnly cookies can be found at http://msdn.microsoft.com/workshop/author/dhtml/httponly_cookies.asp.

Deleting Cookies

```
document.cookie="myLanguage=JavaScript; expires=
➥Thu, 25-Dec-1980 12:34:56 GMT"
```

Setting a cookie value to an empty string effectively
destroys the cookie data, but does not eliminate the
cookie itself. To get rid of a cookie, the expiration date
must be set to some point in the past. Since the UNIX
time measuring starts on January 1, 1970, a date somewhere close to this point is recommended. The preceding code (see deletecookie.html) uses Christmas
1980 as the cookie expiration date. The web browser
sees that this date lies in the past (unless the user
changed the local time settings) and deletes the cookie.
Once again, it is important that the same cookie features are used as when the cookie was set.

Checking for Cookie Support

```
document.cookie="CookieTestTemp=success"
document.cookie="CookieTestPers=success; expires=
➥Tue, 25-Dec-2012 12:34:56 GMT"
```

The only way to actually find out whether a cookie
has been successfully set is by checking for the cookie
upon the next request to the server. However, with
JavaScript, this can be done instantly within one page.
The following code first sets two cookies (a temporary
one and a persistent one) and then checks whether
these two actions were successful. Also, the test cookies
are deleted again—but of course only if setting them
has been successful.

```
<script language="JavaScript"
  type="text/javascript">
document.cookie="CookieTestTemp=success"
document.cookie="CookieTestPers=success; expires=
➥Tue, 25-Dec-2012 12:34:56 GMT"
if (document.cookie.indexOf(
  "CookieTestTemp=success") != -1) {
  window.alert("Temporary cookies are supported!")
  document.cookie="CookieTestTemp=JavaScript;
➥expires=Thu, 25-Dec-1980 12:34:56 GMT"
} else {
  window.alert(
    "Temporary cookies are not supported!")
}
if (document.cookie.indexOf(
  "CookieTestPers=success") != -1) {
  window.alert("Persistent cookies are supported!")
  document.cookie="CookieTestPers=JavaScript;
➥expires=Thu, 25-Dec-1980 12:34:56 GMT"
} else {
  window.alert(
    "Persistent cookies are not supported!")
}
</script>
```

Checking the Browser's Cookie Support (checkcookie.html)

Saving Multiple Information in One Cookie

```
for (var el in data) {
  namevalue += "&" + escape(el) +
    "=" + escape(data[el]);
}
```

Remember the limitations for a cookie-driven site: Only 20 cookies per domain are allowed. Also, if users get a warning when a cookie arrives, the more cookies you send the more annoyed your users will be. Therefore, it can be a clever idea to store more than one bit of information in a cookie.

For this to work, the cookie data must be serialized. There are several different approaches to this, including some really advanced ones. However, if you just want to store a list of name/value pairs, URL encoding is the easiest thing to implement:

```
function serialize(data) {
  var namevalue = "";
  for (var el in data) {
    namevalue += "&" + escape(el) +
                 "=" + escape(data[el]);
  }
  return namevalue.substring(1);
}
```

Serializing an Object (serialize.html; excerpt)

When complex data is used in a cookie, code in the following fashion may be used:

```
document.cookie = "data=" + serialize(myComplexData)
```

The way back requires a bit more code, but consists largely of splitting the data into individual pairs and extracting names and values out of the result:

```
function unserialize(data) {
  var object = new Array();
  var pairs = data.split(/&/g);
  for (var i=0; i<pairs.length; i++) {
```

```
    if (pairs[i].indexOf("=") > -1) {
      object[unescape(pairs[i].substring(
        0, pairs[i].indexOf("=")))] =
        unescape(pairs[i].substring(
        pairs[i].indexOf("=") + 1));
    }
  }
  return object;
}
```

Unserializing an Object (serialize.html; excerpt)

The code file serialize.html serializes and unserializes
an object, without using cookies to make the code a
bit shorter.

NOTE: At http://www.iconico.com/workshop/jsSerializer/, a
more complex serializer is shown that converts an object
into XML. Also, the discussion on JSON from Chapter 11,
"AJAX (and Related Topics)," may be of interest here.

8

Forms

When you're working with server-side technologies, forms are the one aspect of HTML that is most useful since it enables users to "communicate" with the server—by entering data into a form and then submitting that form to the server.

From a JavaScript point of view, HTML forms are very interesting as well. The options HTML is offering are somehow limited, and JavaScript can come to the rescue here. User data must be validated, forms may accept only certain kinds of input, form submission can be possible only when certain requirements are met. All this—and more—is possible with JavaScript, as covered in this chapter.

Understanding HTML Forms with JavaScript

```
document.forms[0]
```

Usually, you access an HTML element using its ID and then document.getElementById(). However, with HTML forms, document.forms is generally used.

One reason for this is that the name attribute of each form element is used when the form is submitted to the server.

`document.forms` is an array of all forms on the current page. So if the form contains only one form, `document.forms[0]` accesses it. Alternatively, forms can also get a name:

```
<form name="mainForm">
...
</form>
```

Then, `document.forms["mainForm"]` accesses the form.

All elements within the form are also referenced by their name, serving as array index for the `elements` property of the form. For instance, imagine that the first form on a page has an element with the attribute `name="element1"`. Then, the following JavaScript code accesses this element:

```
document.forms[0].elements["element1"]
```

There are also shorter versions to access form information. A form named `"mainForm"` and an element `"element1"` allows this shortcut:

```
document.mainForm.element1
```

Generally, the more detailed approach using the `forms` array and especially the `elements` array is used, since this can also be used with automated access to the form elements.

JavaScript can modify form elements, act upon certain events being triggered, and also submit the form (and prevent it from being submitted). Also, JavaScript can come in handy with regard to form data validation. Do, however, always keep in mind that JavaScript can

be deactivated. The form must also work without
JavaScript.

TIP: Every form element supports the form property, which
points to the form the element resides in. Therefore,
this.form is used quite often in the code for form field
elements to grant easy access to the element's form, without having to go through the document.forms array.

Accessing Text Fields

```
window.alert(f.elements["textfield"].value);
```

HTML supports three types of text fields:

- Single-line text fields: `<input type="text" />`
- Multiline text fields: `<textarea></textarea>`
- Password fields: `<input type="password" />`

Although: these fields behave quite differently in a web
browser, access from JavaScript is quite similar. The
value attribute of each of these fields contains the text
within the field. This can be used both for reading and
for writing the field's text.

The following code shows two things: first, how to
access the field's property, and second, how to use
this.form to give easy access to the field's form.

```
<script language="JavaScript"
  type="text/javascript">
function showText(f) {
  window.alert(f.elements["textfield"].value);
}
```

```
</script>
<form>
  <input type="text" name="textfield" />
  <input type="button" value="Show text"
    onclick="showText(this.form);" />
</form>
```

Accessing a Text Field (textfield.html)

Figure 8.1 shows what happens if a user enters some text in the field and then clicks on the button.

Figure 8.1   The text appears after the button is clicked.

NOTE: This approach—using the `value` property to access the data in the form field—also works for hidden fields (`<input type="hidden" />`).

Accessing Check Boxes

```
f.elements["chkbox"].checked ?
  "checked." : "not checked."
```

An HTML check box knows only two states: checked and not checked. So when you're working with

JavaScript, accessing this state is the most commonly used scenario.

The checked property of the check box is a Boolean value returning true if the check box is checked, and false otherwise. The following code shows this in context:

```
<script language="JavaScript"
  type="text/javascript">
function showStatus(f) {
  window.alert("The checkbox is " +
    (f.elements["chkbox"].checked ?
      "checked." : "not checked."));
}
</script>
<form>
  <input type="checkbox" name="chkbox" />
  <input type="button" value="Show status"
    onclick="showStatus(this.form);" />
</form>
```

Accessing a Check Box (checkbox.html)

Accessing Radio Buttons

```
var btn = f.elements["radiobutton"][i];
s += btn.value + ": " + btn.checked + "\n";
```

Unlike check boxes, HTML radio buttons always come in groups. That means that several radio buttons may have the same name attribute, but differ in their value attributes. Therefore, document.forms[*number*].elements[*radiobuttongroup*] accesses the whole group of radio buttons—that is, it is an array. Every sub-element of this array is a radio button and supports the `checked` property. This property works analogous to the check box's `checked` property: `true` means that the radio button is activated, and `false` stands for the opposite.

Access to the value of every button is possible, as well: the `value` property takes care of that.

The following code iterates through all radio buttons and outputs their state:

```
<script language="JavaScript"
  type="text/javascript">
function showStatus(f) {
  var s = "";
  for (var i=0; i<f.elements["radiobutton"].length;
    i++) {
    var btn = f.elements["radiobutton"][i];
    s += btn.value + ": " + btn.checked + "\n";
  }
  window.alert(s);
}
</script>
<form>
  <input type="radio" name="radiobutton"
    value="R" />red
  <input type="radio" name="radiobutton"
    value="G" />green
  <input type="radio" name="radiobutton"
    value="B" />blue
  <input type="button" value="Show status"
    onclick="showStatus(this.form);" />
</form>
```

Accessing a Group of Radio Buttons (radiobutton.html)

Accessing Selection Lists

```
var index = f.elements["selectionlist"]
➡.selectedIndex;
```

An HTML selection list consists of two elements:
<select> lays the foundation and provides the name of
the whole list (in its name attribute). The actual list elements are represented by <option> elements and provide two things: a caption (the data shown in the
browser) and the value (the data sent to the server
when the form is submitted).

When you're working with JavaScript, two ways of
accessing the list data are available:

- selectedIndex provides the index (starting at 0) of
  the currently selected list element; a value of -1
  means that no value has been selected (applicable
  only for lists with size greater than 1).

- options is an array with all list options. Every
  option supports the selected property. When true,
  the list option is selected.

Usually, selectedIndex is good enough for validation
purposes. The options approach comes in quite handy
when the selected list element will be accessed, as well.
Then, the value attribute of the selected option provides the data sent to the server, and the text property
returns the caption visible in the browser.

The following listing accesses all important information regarding the selected option:

```
<script language="JavaScript"
  type="text/javascript">
function showStatus(f) {
```

```
  var index = f.elements["selectionlist"]
➡.selectedIndex;
  if (index == -1) {
    window.alert("No element selected");
  } else {
    var element = f.elements["selectionlist"]
➡.options[index];
    window.alert("Element #" + index +
      " (caption: " + element.text +
      ", value: " + element.value +
      ") selected");
  }
}
</script>
<form>
  <select name="selectionlist" size="3">
    <option value="R">red</option>
    <option value="G">green</option>
    <option value="B">blue</option>
  </select>
  <input type="button" value="Show status"
    onclick="showStatus(this.form);" />
</form>
```

Accessing a Selection List (selectionlist.html)

NOTE: Recent browsers also support the following shortcut for accessing the value of the currently selected list element:

```
f.elements["selectionlist"].value
```

However, to maintain maximum browser compatibility, the following approach requires a bit more typing, but also works on older software:

```
f.elements["selectionlist"].options[
  f.elements["selectionlist"].selectedIndex].value
```

Accessing a Multiple Selection List

```
s += "Element #" + i
  + " (" + option.text
  + "/" + option.value
  + ") " + (option.selected ?
    "selected." : "not selected.")
  + "\n";
```

When an HTML selection list gets the `multiple=
"multiple"` attribute, more than one element can be
selected. In this case, the `selectedIndex` property does
not help very much since it only informs about the
first selected element in the list, not all. Therefore, a `for`
loop should be used to iterate over *all* list elements.
When the `selected` property is `true`, the list item is
selected.

The following code outputs information about all list
elements, including whether or not they are selected:

```
<script language="JavaScript"
  type="text/javascript">
function showStatus(f) {
  var s = "";
  var list = f.elements["selectionlist"];
  for (var i=0; i<list.options.length; i++) {
    var option = list.options[i];
    s += "Element #" + i
      + " (" + option.text
      + "/" + option.value
      + ") " + (option.selected ?
        "selected." : "not selected.")
      + "\n";
  }
  window.alert(s);
```

```
}
</script>
<form>
  <select name="selectionlist" size="3"
    multiple="multiple">
    <option value="R">red</option>
    <option value="G">green</option>
    <option value="B">blue</option>
  </select>
  <input type="button" value="Show status"
    onclick="showStatus(this.form);" />
</form>
```

Accessing a Multiple Selection List (selectionlistmultiple.html)

In Figure 8.2 you can see the result when a few of the elements are selected, but not all.

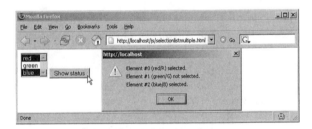

Figure 8.2   Some elements are selected.

File Uploads and JavaScript

With JavaScript it is also possible to access file upload HTML elements (`<input type="file" />`). However, in the past few years, web browser developers have restricted the JavaScript access to these kinds of form fields more and more. And there is good reason for that, too. Imagine a hostile JavaScript code that sets the value of the file upload field to, say, /etc/passwd and then automatically submits the form. Therefore, this is usually not possible any more. Also, some browsers print out a message whenever files will be uploaded alongside a form (see Figure 8.3). Therefore, you should avoid controlling form upload fields with JavaScript; with basic HTML and a server-side technology, they do work fine.

Figure 8.3   Konqueror warns about files being sent with the form.

Disabling Form Elements

```
f.elements["password"].disabled = true;
```

Sometimes, form elements should not be modifiable. The following scenarios are just some examples:

- Form elements "abused" just to display data, such as long license agreements packed into a `<textarea>` field

- Elements being activated or deactivated upon user interaction

- Data in form elements being "locked" when the form is being submitted

JavaScript offers several options to achieve this effect. Every form element supports the `disabled` property. When it's set to `true`, the form element grays out and cannot be modified any longer. In the following listing, this is shown using a simple login form. This form can also be used for registering a user; when a user wants to register, no password is required. Therefore, the password field must gray out when the form switches into registration mode:

```
<script language="JavaScript"
  type="text/javascript">
function enable(f) {
  f.elements["password"].disabled = false;
}

function disable(f) {
  f.elements["password"].disabled = true;
}
</script>
```

```
<form>
  <input type="radio" name="radiobutton"
    value="login"checked="checked"
    onclick="enable(this.form);" />Login
  <input type="radio" name="radiobutton"
    value="register"
    onclick="disable(this.form);" />Register<br />
  Username <input type="text" name="username" />
  <br />
  Password <input type="password"
    name="password" /><br />
</form>
```

Disabling Form Elements (disabled.html)

In Figure 8.4, the effect of this code can be seen: the text field grays out when the Register radio button is selected.

Figure 8.4   The password field is now disabled.

Sometimes, the graying-out effect is not desired. An alternative way to disable a form element comes via its readOnly JavaScript property. When this property is set to true, the form field does not change its appearance, but cannot be changed any longer. Here is the code that implements this:

```
function enable(f) {
  f.elements["password"].readOnly = false;
}

function disable(f) {
  f.elements["password"].readOnly = true;
}
```

Making Form Elements Read-Only (readonly.html; excerpt)

NOTE: In older browsers, another simple trick was used to make text fields in particular read-only. After the field got the focus, it was removed immediately:

```
<input type="text" onfocus="this.blur();" />
```

WARNING: Even though you can use JavaScript to disable a form field or make it read-only, you should be aware that JavaScript can be easily deactivated and an HTTP request can be trivially forged, as well. So do not rely on this JavaScript effect but always validate your data on the server side!

Submitting a Form

```
document.forms[0].submit();
```

Usually, a submit button (`<input type="submit" />`) or a submit image (`<input type="image" />`) is used to send form data to the web server. However, JavaScript is capable of submitting a form as well, using the form's `submit()` method. This allows programmers to use an HTML link, for instance, to submit a form, providing more flexibility from a designer's point of view. However, do keep in mind that the following code works only when JavaScript is activated:

```
<form>
  <input type="hidden" name="field" value="data" />
</form>
<a href="javascript:document.forms[0].submit();">
➥Submit form</a>
```

Submitting a Form (submit.html)

Preventing Form Submission

```
<form onsubmit="return checkform(this);">
```

There are some good reasons to hinder the browser from submitting the form, for instance, when some required fields have not been filled out yet. To do so, `false` must be returned in the handling code for the form's `submit` event:

```
<form onsubmit="return false;">
```

Of course, the code should usually decide based on the form data whether the form should be allowed to submit. Therefore, a custom function usually takes care of that and, at the end, returns `true` or `false`.

The following form can be submitted only if there is a value in the text field:

```
<script language="JavaScript"
  type="text/javascript">
function checkform(f) {
```

```
  if (f.elements["textfield"].value == "") {
    return false;
  } else {
    return true;
  }
}
</script>
<form onsubmit="return checkform(this);">
  Username <input type="text" name="textfield" />
  <input type="submit" value="Submit data" />
</form>
```

The Form Can Be Submitted Only When the Text Field Is Filled Out (nosubmit.html)

Once again, this works only with JavaScript activated—one more reason to validate all data on the server side!

Preventing Repeated Form Submissions

```
<form action="delay.php">
  <input type="submit" value="Submit data"
    onclick="this.disabled = true;"/>
</form>
```

Especially when the script that analyzes form data takes quite some time, users tend to try to speed things up by submitting the form again. However, during online shopping, credit-card payments, and other important transactions, this can be quite expensive. Therefore, the web page itself should try to avoid repeated form submissions.

The preceding code (in the file prevent.html in the code downloads for this title) does exactly that: When the submit button has been clicked, the button's disabled property is set to true, effectively making it impossible to click the button again (if JavaScript is enabled). Figure 8.5 shows the result in the browser: The button grays out.

Figure 8.5   The button cannot be clicked twice.

The preceding listing and the following listing both send the form data to a PHP script called delay.php, which basically waits five seconds and then sends out data. This emulates a slow connection or a slow server, the main scenario for this phrase.

Another approach is to maintain the state of the button and thereby determine whether it has already been clicked, as the following listing shows:

```
<script language="JavaScript"
  type="text/javascript">
var submitted = false;
function checkform(f) {
  if (submitted) {
    window.alert("Form has already been
➡submitted!");
    return false;
```

```
  } else {
    submitted = true;
    return true;
  }
}
</script>
<form action="delay.php"
  onsubmit="return checkform(this);">
  <input type="submit" value="Submit data" />
</form>
```

*Preventing a Repeated Form Submission Maintaining a Status
(prevent-status.html)*

WARNING: Although this phrase is quite convenient, you
have to be aware that sometimes the server unexpectedly
closes the connection to the client (or vice versa). Then the
data transfer stops, but the JavaScript code cannot know
about this. The consequence is that the button cannot be
clicked twice (as originally planned), but the data has not
been properly transmitted. The user then would have to
reload the form to be able to submit the data again.

Giving a Field the Focus

```
document.forms[0].elements["textfield"].focus();
```

Most search websites like Google have a convenient
feature: After the page has been loaded, the cursor is
already in the search field. This is quite easily done by
the preceding code; the focus() method gives a form
field the focus. A full listing is available in the file
focus.html.

> **WARNING:** Note that the larger your page is and the
> more form fields it has, the more inconvenient this feature
> may get. Imagine a slowly loading page. While the page is
> loading, the user is probably already typing in another
> field. After the page has been fully loaded, the preceding
> code sets the focus to the designated field, eventually
> stealing the focus from the field the user is currently
> working on.

Selecting Text in a Field

```
field.setSelectionRange(0, field.value.length);
```

Sometimes, text fields are prefilled with text explaining
to the user what is expected in the field, for instance,
in the following fashion:

```
<input type="text" name="textfield"
  value="&lt;Enter data here&gt;" />
```

However, this is a bit cumbersome when users try to
actually enter something in the field: They have to
select the whole text to be able to overwrite the field's
contents. If the text was preselected, this would be easy.

All major browsers support selecting text in a field;
however, the approach is different. With Internet
Explorer, the `createTextRange()` method of the field
must be called, creating a range. The `moveStart()` and
`moveEnd()` methods define the delimiters of this range;
the `select()` method finally selects the text.

Mozilla browsers and Opera and Konqueror/KDE, on
the other hand, have a different interface for this functionality. The `setSelectionRange()` method selects a
field's contents. Note that `setSelectionRange()` expects

the length of the range as second parameter, whereas moveEnd() in Internet Explorer expects the position of the last character to select.

The following listing selects the whole text in all major browsers and then sets the focus on the field. So if the user starts typing, the initial text is replaced immediately.

```
<script language="JavaScript"
  type="text/javascript">
window.onload = function() {
  var field = document.forms[0]
➡.elements["textfield"];
  if (field.createTextRange) {
    var range = field.createTextRange();
    range.moveStart("character", .0);
    range.moveEnd("character",
      field.value.length - 1);
    range.select();
  } else if (field.setSelectionRange) {
    field.setSelectionRange(0, field.value.length);
  }
  field.focus();
};
</script>
<form>
  <input type="text" name="textfield"
    value="&lt;Enter data here&gt;" />
</form>
```

Preselecting Text in a Field (selecttext.html)

Figure 8.6 shows the result. Note that when this form field is validated later, the default value should not be considered as valid data.

Figure 8.6   The text is selected, and the field
has the focus.

TIP: You may consider prefilling the field only if JavaScript
is available; otherwise, users without JavaScript would
have to manually select (and delete) the standard value of
the text field. The following code does the trick:

field.value = "<Enter data here>";

Emptying Text Fields When Clicked Upon

```
if (this.value == originaldata) {
  this.value = "";
}
```

A nice additional feature to the preceding phrase is to
clear out the text field if the user clicks into it (because
then, the preselection of the text would be gone).
However, just adding onclick="this.value='';" to the
<input> tag would not be enough. Imagine that the
user entered some custom data into the field and then
decided to click in it—the text would vanish, and the
user probably would too.

Therefore, the original text has to be saved upon loading of the page. Now when the user clicks in the text

field and the text in it is still the original, the field may be emptied, as the following listing shows:

```
<script language="JavaScript"
  type="text/javascript">
var originaldata;

window.onload = function() {
  var field = document.forms[0]
➥.elements["textfield"];
  originaldata = field.value;
  if (field.createTextRange) {
    var range = field.createTextRange();
    range.moveStart("character", .0);
    range.moveEnd("character",
      field.value.length - 1);
    range.select();
  } else if (field.setSelectionRange) {
    field.setSelectionRange(0, field.value.length);
  }
  field.focus();
  field.onclick = function() {
    if (this.value == originaldata) {
      this.value = "";
    }
  };
}
</script>
<form>
  <input type="text" name="textfield"
    value="&lt;Enter data here&gt;" />
</form>
```

Clearing the Field (clear.html)

Note that the focus event cannot be used for that task; Internet Explorer would clear out the field immediately upon loading of the document (even though the call to focus() occurs before the event handler is set).

Form Validation

JavaScript is a great tool for validating forms on the fly. It is possible to give users immediate feedback about data they entered (for instance, by using something along the lines of onblur="validateData(this);"), but you have to always consider that JavaScript can be deactivated and HTTP requests must not originate from a web browser. So before you use data from the client, validate it on the server as well.

Also, make sure that the form itself works with JavaScript deactivated, since about 10% of users cannot use the scripting language (or do not want to).

Finally, validation itself should be only a convenience feature for users, not a nagging tool to squeeze as much data out of a visitor as possible. So use it wisely.

Validating Text Fields

```
if (field.value.replace(/\s/g, "") == "") {
  window.alert("Invalid data!");
  field.focus();
```

Validation of user-supplied data can come in various flavors. Sometimes it is just important to check whether a mandatory field has been filled out; in other scenarios a thorough data validation has to be done.

In the preceding code (file mandatory.html), the data in a text field is checked. The replace() JavaScript method call globally removes whitespace (regular expression /\s/g) in the string and then checks if there is anything left, so that just space characters do not satisfy the "fill out this field" condition.

In the next listing, the data in the text field is validated against a regular expression—a U.S. postal code:

```
<script language="JavaScript"
  type="text/javascript">
function validate(field) {
  var regex = /^\d{5}$/;
  if (!regex.test(field.value)) {
    window.alert("Invalid postal code!");
    field.value = "";
    field.focus();
  }
}
</script>
<form onsubmit="return checkform(this);">
  US postal code <input type="text" name="code"
                    onblur="validate(this);" />
</form>
```

Validating a Field Against a Regular Expression
(mandatory-regex.html)

Validating Check Boxes

```
if (!f.elements["terms"].checked) {
  window.alert("Terms &amp; conditions must be
Âaccepted!");
  f.elements["terms"].focus();
  return false;
} else {
  return true;
}
```

When a check box has to be filled out, its `checked` property must be `true`; otherwise, the form should not be allowed to be submitted. The preceding code, available in a full listing in the file `mandatory-checkbox.html`, demonstrates which code could be called when the `submit` event of the form is fired.

Validating Radio Buttons

```
if (radio.checked) {
  return true;
}
```

When a group of radio buttons is mandatory, it suffices that *one* of these buttons is checked (well, it is not possible to check more than one button per group anyway, but there is still the possibility that *none* of the buttons is selected). Using the `elements` array of the form, the group of radio buttons can be selected as an array. Within this array, at least one radio button with `checked` equals `true` must be found so that the group is considered to be sufficiently filled out. The following listing implements this check:

```
<script language="JavaScript"
  type="text/javascript">
function checkform(f) {
  for (var i=0; i<f.elements["colors"].length;
    i++) {
    var radio = f.elements["colors"][i];
    if (radio.checked) {
      return true;
    }
  }
  // no checked radio button found
```

```
  window.alert("No color selected!");
  f.elements["colors"][0].focus();
  return false;
}
</script>
<form onsubmit="return checkform(this);">
  <input type="radio" name="colors" value="R" />
➥red<br />
  <input type="radio" name="colors" value="G" />
➥green<br />
  <input type="radio" name="colors" value="B" />
➥blue<br />
  <input type="submit" value="Submit data" />
</form>
```

Validating a Radio Button Group (mandatory-radio.html)

NOTE: You may want to consider a less obtrusive way of pointing the user to the error in the form. For instance, you could use DOM or the Image object to display a small error icon next to all fields that have not been correctly filled out. This is, of course, a possibility for all validation phrases in this chapter.

Validating Selection Lists

```
if (f.elements["colors"].selectedIndex == -1) {
  window.alert("No color selected!");
  f.elements["colors"].focus();
  return false;
} else {
  return true;
}
```

There are several ways to validate a selection list. The easiest one is to check the `selectedIndex` property. If its value is -1, no item has been selected, and therefore the form has not been filled out sufficiently. The preceding code demonstrates this (full version in file `mandatory-list.html`).

However, this approach works only when the selection list has its `size` attribute set to a value greater than one and does not contain any empty elements (for demonstration purposes). A better way to validate a list is to look at the `value` attributes of all selected elements. If the value is an empty string, the element is not taken into consideration. A `for` loop iterates over all elements in the list and looks for selected elements with an actual value. This approach has the additional advantage that it also works with multiple selection lists.

```
<script language="JavaScript"
  type="text/javascript">
function checkform(f) {
  for (var i=0; i<f.elements["colors"].options
➥.length; i++) {
    var element = f.elements["colors"].options[i];
    if (element.selected && element.value != "") {
      return true;
    }
  }
  window.alert("No color selected!");
  f.elements["colors"].focus();
  return false;
}
</script>
<form onsubmit="return checkform(this);">
  <select name="colors" size="9"
    multiple="multiple">
```

```
    <option value="">Select a color</option>
    <option value="R">red</option>
    <option value="G">green</option>
    <option value="B">blue</option>
    <option value="">-----</option>
    <option value="C">cyan</option>
    <option value="M">magenta</option>
    <option value="Y">yellow</option>
    <option value="K">black</option>
  </select>
  <input type="submit" value="Submit data" />
</form>
```

Validating a Selection List (mandatory-list-loop.html)

As you can see from Figure 8.7, the two filler elements do not count.

Figure 8.7   The form may be submitted only if a "real" element has been selected.

Automatically Validating a Form

```
switch (element.type)
```

With a bit of effort, JavaScript is capable of automatically validating a form, given that all form fields are mandatory. Then, iterating over the form elements does the trick. Each element's `type` property returns the type of the field, and Table 8.1 shows a list of the most important ones. Then, depending on the field type, the validation takes place.

Table 8.1   The Form Field Types of JavaScript

Type	Description
button	HTML button
checkbox	Check box
password	Password field
radio	Radio button
reset	Reset button
select-one	Selection list
select-multiple	Multiple selection list
submit	Submit button
text	Single-line text field
textarea	Multiline text field

The following code takes special care of radio button groups. Since the loop over the form elements visits every element and therefore every radio button, a list of already-checked radio button groups is maintained.

Otherwise, a group of three radio buttons would be checked three times, generating three error messages if no button has been selected.

```javascript
<script language="JavaScript"
  type="text/javascript">
function checkform(f) {
  var errortext = "";
  var checkedgroups = "";
  for (var i=0; i<f.elements.length; i++) {
    var element = f.elements[i];
    switch (element.type) {
      case "text":
      case "textarea":
      case "password":
        if (element.value.replace(/\s/g, "") ==
          "") {
          errortext += element.name + "\n";
        }
        break;
      case "checkbox":
        if (!element.checked) {
          errortext += element.name + "\n";
        }
        break;
      case "radio":
        var group = f.elements[element.name];
        if (checkedgroups.indexOf("[" +
          element.name + "]") > -1) {
          continue;
        } else {
          checkedgroups += "[" + element.name + "]";
        }
        var groupok = false;
        for (var j=0; j<group.length; j++) {
          if (group[j].checked) {
```

```
            groupok = true;
          }
        }
        if (!groupok) {
          errortext += element.name + "\n";
        }
        break;
      case "select-one":
      case "select-multiple":
        var selectok = false;
        for (var j=0; j<element.options.length;
          j++) {
          var item = element.options[j];
          if (item.selected && item.value != "") {
            selectok = true;
          }
        }
        if (!selectok) {
          errortext += element.name + "\n";
        }
        break;
    }
  }
  if (errortext == "") {
    return true;
  } else {
    window.alert(
      "The following fields have not been correctly
➥filled out:\n\n"
      + errortext);
    return false;
  }
}
</script>
```

Automatically Validating a Form (validate.html; excerpt)

Figure 8.8 presents the result: All form fields miss their appropriate content. Note, though, that you may want to amend this script and maybe exclude check boxes from the list, since these form elements are optional most of the time.

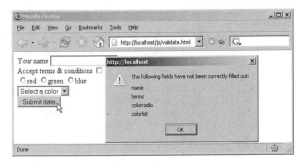

Figure 8.8   The form is automatically validated.

Implementing Navigation with a Selection List

```
var url = list.options[list.selectedIndex].value;
```

A so-called "quick link" navigation presents a selection list with a couple of navigation elements. After an item in the list has been selected, the browser loads the associated page.

Implementation-wise, this nice and widely used effect is rather trivial. The target URLs of all navigation elements are stored in the value attributes; a JavaScript function first checks whether a "real" element has been selected and then loads the URL:

```
<script language="JavaScript"
  type="text/javascript">
function loadURL(list) {
  var url = list.options[list.selectedIndex].value;
  if (url != "") {
    location.href = url;
  }
}
</script>
<form>
  <select name="urls" onchange="loadURL(this);">
    <option value="">Please select...</option>
    <option value="http://www.samspublishing.com/">
➥SAMS</option>
    <option value="http://www.hauser-wenz.de/blog/">
➥H&amp;W blog</option>
    <option value="http://www.damonjordan.com/">
➥Damon</option>
  </select>
</form>
```

A Quick Link Navigation (quicklink.html)

Implementing a Hierarchical Navigation with a Selection List

```
for (var i=0; i<links.length; i++) {
  elements["urls"].options[
    elements["urls"].options.length] =
      new Option(links[i].title, links[i].url);
}
```

Two selection lists can be paired to provide a hierarchical navigation on a site. The first selection list contains several categories; when a category is selected, the second list contains a set of elements in this category.

From a JavaScript point of view, a list of elements must be maintained and the lists must be filled according to the selection in the first (category) list. So here is the list of links, in JSON format (see Chapter 11, "AJAX (and Related Topics)" for more information on this notation).

```javascript
var data = {
  "search" : [
    {"title": "Google", "url":
➥"http://www.google.com/"},
    {"title": "MSN", "url":
➥"http://search.msn.com/"}
  ],
  "browsers" : [
    {"title": "Firefox",
➥"url": "http://www.mozilla.com/firefox/"},
    {"title": "Opera",
➥"url": "http://www.opera.com/"}
  ]
};
```

Then, the following code adds options to the second selection list, by using the Option constructor (syntax: first the caption, then the value):

```javascript
<script language="JavaScript"
  type="text/javascript">
function loadElements(f) {
  with (f) {
    var category = elements["categories"].options[
      elements["categories"].selectedIndex].value;
    if (category != "") {
      var links = data[category];
```

```
      elements["urls"].options.length = 0;
      elements["urls"].options[0] =
        new Option("Please select...", "#");
      for (var i=0; i<links.length; i++) {
        elements["urls"].options[
          elements["urls"].options.length] =
          new Option(links[i].title, links[i].url);
      }
    }
  }
}
</script>
<form>
  <select name="categories"
    onchange="loadElements(this.form);">
    <option value="">Please select...</option>
    <option value="search">Search Engines</option>
    <option value="browsers">Browsers</option>
  </select>
  <select name="urls" onchange="loadURL(this);">
  </select>
</form>
```

A Hierarchical Navigation (navigation.html; excerpt)

Figure 8.9 shows what happens when the first category (search engines) is selected: The second list fills with available options.

Figure 8.9 Selecting an option in the first list fills the second list.

Emptying a Set of Radio Buttons

```
for (var i=0; i<f.elements["colors"].length; i++) {
  f.elements["colors"][i].checked = false;
}
```

One commonly known disadvantage of radio buttons is that after a button in a group is selected, it is impossible to remove the selection from the group—at least one button is always selected from then on. With a little bit of JavaScript, this effect can be mitigated by offering a JavaScript button or link that removes the radio button selection. The preceding code iterates over the radio button group and sets the `checked` property of all elements to `false` (complete code in the file `emptyradio.html`).

TIP: This issue can also be solved by HTML alone: Just offer a radio button (selected by default) that stands for "no selection," in the following fashion:

```
<input type="radio" name="answer" value="Y" />yes
<input type="radio" name="answer" value="N" />no
<input type="radio" name="answer" value=""
  checked="checked" />no answer
```

Of course, you would then also have to change any validation code.

Creating Prefilled Date Selection Lists

```
elements["day"].selectedIndex = d.getDate() - 1;
```

Most online booking sites have a set of three selection lists allowing users to enter a date: one list for the day, one for the month, and one for the year. Generating these lists, either in static HTML or on the server side, is a rather trivial task; but preselecting them requires server-side means (see the book *PHP Phrasebook* for a solution in PHP)—or a bit of JavaScript. The idea is to set the selectedIndex property of each list to the appropriate date value, as shown in the following listing (the selection lists are of course abridged):

```
<script language="JavaScript"
  type="text/javascript">
window.onload = function() {
  with (document.forms[0]) {
    var d = new Date();
    elements["day"].selectedIndex = d.getDate() - 1;
    elements["month"].selectedIndex = d.getMonth();
    elements["year"].selectedIndex = 2006 -
      d.getFullYear();
  }
}
</script>
<form>
  <select name="day">
    <option value="1">1</option>
    <!- ... ->
  </select>
  <select name="month">
    <option value="1">January</option>
```

```
   <!- ... ->
 </select>
 <select name="year">
   <option value="2006">2006</option>
   <!- ... ->
 </select>
</form>
```

Prefilling a Date List (autodate.html; excerpt)

WARNING: In the example, the first year in the list is 2006; this value is also used for calculating the required selectedIndex for that date. If you change that, for instance add the year 2007, you have to change the formula for elements["year"].selectedIndex accordingly.

Creating Validating Date Selection Lists

`f.elements["day"].options.length = maxDays;`

The next step for the date selection lists from the previous phrase consists of taking care of users entering a valid date. So, whenever there is a change in the month or in the year, the day selection list must be updated appropriately:

```
<select name="month"
  onchange="updateDay(this.form);">
<select name="year"
  onchange="updateDay(this.form);">
```

To do so, a helper function (see Chapter 6) determines whether a year is a leap year:

```
function isLeapYear(y) {
  return (y % 4 == 0 &&
    (y % 100 != 0 || y % 400 == 0));
}
```

With this information, the day selection list can be updated. If there are too many entries, the list is shortened. If there are too few entries, the list gets additional entries. All this maintains the selectedIndex value, if possible, so that the user's selection is maintained (unless, for instance, day 30 is selected and the month changed to February).

```
<script language="JavaScript"
  type="text/javascript">
function updateDay(f) {
  var oldDays = f.elements["day"].options.length;
  var month = parseInt(f.elements["month"].value);
  var year = parseInt(f.elements["year"].value);

  var maxDays = 30;

  switch (month) {
    case 1: case 3: case 5: case 7: case 9: case 11:
      maxDays = 31;
      break;
    case 2:
      maxDays = (isLeapYear(year) ? 29 : 28);
      break;
  }

  f.elements["day"].options.length = maxDays;
  if (maxDays > oldDays) {
    for (var i=oldDays; i<maxDays; i++) {
      f.elements["day"].options[i] =
        new Option(i+1, i+1);
```

```
    }
  }
}
</script>
```

Automatically Updating the List (date.html; excerpt)

In Figure 8.10 you can see the result: February of the year 2000 had 29 days.

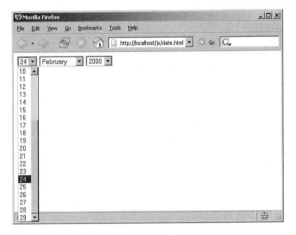

Figure 8.10 The day list is updated according to month and year.

9

Windows and Frames

Windows are playing an important role in JavaScript. The window object is the default object in JavaScript and is used quite often (just consider the windows.alert() method). Also, JavaScript is capable of working with windows (for instance, by opening new ones)—and also with frames and iframes, which are also very similar to window objects.

```
window.open("http://www.samspublishing.com/",
  "samsWindow", "");
```

The method window.open() opens a new window and expects at least three parameters so that the method call is useful: the URL to open, the new name of the window, and window options.

With the preceding code (file open.html), a new window is opened with the publisher's homepage opened.

The second parameter of the open() method provides the name of the new window. This works exactly as a frame name: If you use the window name as the target attribute for a link, the link opens in the new window.

Therefore, the open.html sample file also contains a link that is using the new window name:

```
<a href="http://www.amazon.com/gp/product/
➥0672328801" target="samsWindow">This book
➥at Amazon</a>
```

When you click on that link, no new window is opened but the old window, previously opened by JavaScript, is reused.

Note that the return value of window.open() is a JavaScript window object pointing to the new window. So code in the following fashion does not lead to the desired result:

```
<a href="javascript:window.open(...)">Open
window</a>
```

Since the method returns a window object, this link would write something like [object] (Internet Explorer) or [object Window] (Mozilla browsers) to the page. Therefore, you must make sure that the JavaScript code does not return anything. A good way to achieve this is via the following code:

```
<a href="javascript:void(window.open(...))">Open
➥window</a>
```

Using Window Options

```
window.open("http://www.samspublishing.com/",
    "samsWindow",
    "width=640,height=480,directories=no,menubar=no,
➥toolbar=no,scrollbars=yes");
```

The third parameter of window.open() is a list of comma-separated values that define how the new window looks. You can define the size (as long as both width and height are at least 100 pixels), toggle some window features like the status bar, and more. Table 9.1 shows the most important options (however, the list is not complete, leaving out several browser-dependent options).

The preceding code uses some of these options. Some take numeric values; some require yes or no as their values. Take care that you do not use spaces between options.

Table 9.1   Window Options

Option	Description
dependent	Closes the new window if the parent window is closed
directories	Toggles the personal toolbar
height	Height of the window
innerHeight	Height of the window excluding the window decoration (non-IE only)
innerWidth	Width of the window excluding the window decoration (non-IE only)
left	Horizontal position of the window (IE only)
location	Toggles the location bar
menubar	Toggles the menu bar
outerHeight	Height of the window (non-IE only)
outerWidth	Width of the window (non-IE only)
resizeable	Whether the window may be resized by the user

Table 9.1 **Continued**

Option	Description
screenX	Horizontal position of the window (non-IE only)
screenY	Vertical position of the window (non-IE only)
scrollbars	Toggles the scrollbars
status	Toggles the status bar
toolbar	Toggles the toolbar
top	Vertical position of the window (IE only)
width	Width of the window
z-lock	Gives the window a lower z-lock (position on the z axis) value

WARNING: You cannot expect all of these effects to work on all browsers in an identical fashion. For instance, the Opera browser opens a new window not in a new browser window, but (depending on the browser version) in a new tab, which of course has the default window decoration and the default window size.

Figure 9.1 shows how the newly opened window (file openoptions.html) looks with the given options.

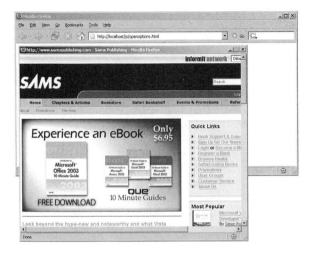

Figure 9.1   The new window has only very
little decoration.

Opening a Modal Window

```
window.showModalDialog(
  "http://www.samspublishing.com/",
  "samsWindow",
  "dialogWidth=640,dialogHeight=480,status=no,
➥center=yes");
```

Both major browsers support some proprietary extensions to the window object, but for obvious reasons
these are not covered here. However, there is one
exception: Internet Explorer is capable of creating
modal windows, something that is quite common in
intranet applications in which the browser type can be
mandated by the IT staff.

The method associated with that is window.
showModalDialog(), expecting a URL, a name, and a set
of options (which you will find listed in Table 9.2).

The following listing opens such a dialog, centers it,
and gives it a size of 640×480 pixels.

```
<script language="JavaScript"
  type="text/javascript">
if (window.showModalDialog) {
  window.showModalDialog(
    "http://www.samspublishing.com/",
    "samsWindow",
    "dialogWidth=640,dialogHeight=480,status=no,
➥center=yes");
}
</script>
<a href="http://www.amazon.com/gp/product/
➥0672328801" target="samsWindow">This
➥book at Amazon</a>
```

Opening a Modal Window (modal.html)

Table 9.2   Window Options

Option	Description
center	Centers the window
dialogHeight	Height of the window
dialogLeft	Horizontal position of the window
dialogTop	Vertical position of the window
dialogWidth	Width of the window
help	Toggles the help symbol in the top-right corner
status	Toggles the status bar
resizeable	Whether the window may be resized by the user

Figure 9.2 shows the modal window produced by the preceding code.

Figure 9.2   The modal window (Internet Explorer only).

Determining Screen Size

```
window.alert(screen.availWidth + " x " +
             screen.availHeight + " pixels");
```

In an ideal world, all web layouts would be flexible and would adapt to the currently available solution. Unfortunately, this is not the case, but you may be able to adapt with JavaScript.

The screen object (window.screen in recent browsers; just screen in older ones) provides information about the current screen resolution. The properties you will be interested in are `availableHeight` and `availableWidth`, providing the height and the width available. This can, for instance, be used for determining the current resolution and redirecting to a page suitable for those screen dimensions.

The preceding code (file `screen.html`) determines the current available screen space. Figure 9.3 shows the result using a 1024×768-pixel solution.

Figure 9.3   The screen dimensions may not be what you expected.

NOTE: Note that in the specific example 30 pixels are missing—they "belong" to the Microsoft Windows bar (similar effects are achieved when this code sample is run on other systems with system bars). If you are interested in the actual width and height, use the `width` and `height` properties of the `screen` object.

Determining the Window Size

```
with (document.body) {
  window.alert(clientWidth + " x " +
              clientHeight + " pixels");
}
```

Accessing the properties of the current window largely depends on the browser used. As is often the case with

JavaScript, the browser world is divided into two groups: Internet Explorer and the rest. With Internet Explorer, the width of a window can be determined via `document.body.clientWidth`; other browsers use `window.innerWidth` for the "inner" width (excluding window decoration) and `window.outerWidth` for the "outer" width (including window decoration). For determining the height, just replace width and Width with height and Height, respectively.

The following code outputs the current window's dimensions:

```
<script language="JavaScript"
  type="text/javascript">
window.onload = function() {
  if (window.innerWidth) {
    window.alert("inner: " + window.innerWidth +
      " x " + window.innerHeight +
      " pixels\nouter: " + window.outerWidth +
      " x " + window.outerHeight + " pixels");
  } else {
    with (document.body) {
      window.alert(clientWidth + " x " +
        clientHeight + " pixels");
    }
  }
}
</script>
<body></body>
```

Determining the Current Window's Dimensions (dimensions.html)

TIP: Note that the page needs a <body> area and the code must not be executed before the page has been fully loaded for the code to work in Internet Explorer.

Resizing a Window

```
window.resizeTo(640, 480);
```

There are several ways to set a window's size. When
opening a window using window.open(), you just have
to set the width and height options. For existing windows, however, JavaScript offers two methods of the
window object:

- resizeTo() sets the width and the height of the
  window to the provided values, as the preceding
  code (file resizeto.html in the download archive)
  shows.

- resizeBy() changes the width and the height of
  the window by adding the provided values, as the
  following listing shows (which cuts both the
  width and the height in half):

```
<script language="JavaScript"
  type="text/javascript">
window.onload = function() {
  var width, height;
  if (window.innerWidth) {
    width = window.outerWidth;
    height = window.outerHeight;
  } else {
    width = document.body.clientWidth;
    height = document.body.clientHeight;
  }
  window.resizeBy(
    -Math.round(width / 2),
    -Math.round(height / 2));
}
```

```
</script>
<body></body>
```

Bisecting a Window's Width and Height (resizeby.html)

WARNING: Resizing a window is considered more or less unfriendly. One of the principles of the Web is that the size of the client is irrelevant and can be adjusted by the user. So use the technique in this phrase wisely. Also note that you cannot resize the window to a width or height lower than 100 pixels.

Repositioning a Window

```
window.moveBy(-10, 10);
```

When opening a new window, you have to take all browsers into account: For Internet Explorer, set the left and top options; all other browsers work with screenX and screenY. The following window.open() call creates a window in the top-left corner of the screen.

```
window.open(
  "anypage.html",
  "name",
  "left=0,top=0,screenX=0,screenY=0");
```

However, for existing windows, two methods that are quite similar to the previous phrase come into play:

- moveTo() positions the window at the specified place, as the code at the beginning of this phrase (in file moveto.html) shows.

- moveBy() moves the window by a certain delta.
  The following listing moves the window 10 pixels
  to the left and 10 pixels down.

```
<script language="JavaScript"
  type="text/javascript">
window.moveBy(-10, 10);
</script>
```

Moving a Window (moveby.html)

WARNING: Moving a window is almost as unfriendly as
resizing it, so once again, use this capability wisely. Also
note that you cannot move the window completely out of
the user's sight, for obvious security reasons.

Opening a Centered Pop-Up Window

```
newwin.moveTo(
  Math.round((screenwidth - windowwidth) / 2),
  Math.round((screenheight - windowheight) / 2));
```

Combining the phrases to open a window, determining its dimensions, and repositioning it enable you to
create a new window that is centered on the page.

The idea is to calculate the width and height of the
new window (remember that window.open() returns a
reference to the new window) and then determine the
screen size, and from that to calculate the required
position of the window so that it is centered.

However, timing is crucial here. On Internet Explorer
you can access the window dimensions only after the
<body> element has been parsed. Therefore, a small
trick is used: First, the new window is empty. Then,
document.write() creates a <body> element. Then, the
window width and height can be read. Finally, the
desired document is loaded in the new window, which
is then repositioned to the center of the screen.

```
<script language="JavaScript"
  type="text/javascript">
var newwin = window.open("", "samsWindow", "");
newwin.document.write("<body></body>");

var windowwidth, windowheight;
if (window.innerWidth) {
  windowwidth = newwin.outerWidth;
  windowheight = newwin.outerHeight;
} else {
  windowwidth = newwin.document.body.clientWidth;
  windowheight = newwin.document.body.clientHeight;
}
var screenwidth = screen.availWidth;
var screenheight = screen.availHeight;
newwin.moveTo(
  Math.round((screenwidth - windowwidth) / 2),
  Math.round((screenheight - windowheight) / 2));
newwin.location.href =
  "http://www.samspublishing.com/";
</script>
<body></body>
```

Opening and Centering a Window (center.html)

NOTE: Sometimes, reading the window properties does not work as planned in Internet Explorer and yields false results. In that case, it is better to set the size of the new window in the `window.open()` call and then use this (known as true) value to center the new window.

Opening a Full-Screen Window

```
newwin.resizeTo(screen.width, screen.height);
newwin.moveTo(0, 0);
```

Internet Explorer 4 supports the `window.open()` option `fullscreen=yes`, but a more general approach is of course to read out the screen object for the system's dimensions and then resize the window appropriately. Do not forget to reposition it in the top-left corner of the screen!

```
<script language="JavaScript"
  type="text/javascript">
var newwin = window.open(
  "http://www.samspublishing.com/",
  "samsWindow",
  "directories=no,menubar=no,toolbar=no,
➥scrollbars=yes");
newwin.resizeTo(screen.width, screen.height);
newwin.moveTo(0, 0);
</script>
```

Opening a Full-Screen Window (center.html)

Opening a New Window in a Corner of the Screen

```
newwin.moveTo(
  screenwidth - windowwidth,
  screenheight - windowheight);
```

Opening a window in the top-left corner of the screen is rather easy: Just provide 0 as the horizontal and vertical position:

```
<script language="JavaScript"
  type="text/javascript">
var newwin = window.open(
  "http://www.samspublishing.com/",
  "samsWindow",
  "width=640,height=480,directories=no,menubar=no,
➥toolbar=no,scrollbars=yes,left=0,top=0,screenX=0,
➥screenY=0");
</script>
```

Opening a Window in the Top-Left Corner (open_topleft.html)

All other corners on the screen are a bit more difficult since you have to calculate the positions. Thanks to the screen object, this dilemma can be solved with a small amount of code. The following code positions the new window in the bottom-left corner; listings for the other two corners are available in the files open_topright.html and open_bottomleft.html.

```
<script language="JavaScript"
  type="text/javascript">
var newwin = window.open(
  "http://www.samspublishing.com/",
```

```
  "samsWindow",
  "width=640,height=480,directories=no,menubar=no,
➥toolbar=no,scrollbars=yes");
var windowwidth = 640;
var windowheight = 480;
var screenwidth = screen.availWidth;
var screenheight = screen.availHeight;
newwin.moveTo(
  screenwidth - windowwidth,
  screenheight - windowheight);
</script>
```

Opening a Window in the Bottom-Right Corner
(open_bottomright.html)

Creating a Sitemap

```
this.opener.name = "mainWindow";
```

A sitemap is very convenient on any website. With a
bit of JavaScript, this feature can get even better.

If you open a sitemap in a new window, you of course
want all the links in a sitemap to open up in the original window. Obviously, this can be done by setting
the target attribute of all HTML links (or use
<base target="..." />). However, one question
remains: Which is the window name? One way to
answer this question is to use JavaScript in the main
window and set the window's name property:

```
this.name = "mainWindow";
```

Another way is to use the sitemap and reference the
opening window from there. This is done by the

opener property of the window, which is set to the
parent window of the current window (if there is any
parent). The following code is the complete sitemap:

```
<script language="JavaScript"
  type="text/javascript">
this.opener.name = "mainWindow";
</script>
<a href="http://www.samspublishing.com/"
  target="mainWindow">Publisher</a><br />
<a href="http://www.amazon.com/gp/product/
➥0672328801" target="mainWindow">This
➥book at Amazon</a>
```

The Sitemap (sitemapwindow.html; excerpt)

And this listing opens the sitemap:

```
<script language="JavaScript"
  type="text/javascript">
window.open(
  "sitemapwindow.html",
  "sitemap",
  "width=320,height=100,directories=no,menubar=no,
➥toolbar=no,scrollbars=yes");
</script>
```

Opening the Sitemap (sitemap.html; excerpt)

Closing a Window

```
if (!newwindow.closed) newwindow.close();
```

Closing a window can be done by calling the window's close() method. However, by default this is

possible only for windows that were opened using
JavaScript; if you try this on other windows, the user
gets a warning message similar to the one shown in
Figure 9.4 (Mozilla browsers have a similar message,
but hide it in the JavaScript console).

Figure 9.4   Close only the windows opened with
JavaScript—or cope with this frightening message.

With the sitemap from the previous phrase, a link to
close the window comes in handy:

```
<script language="JavaScript"
  type="text/javascript">
this.opener.name = "mainWindow";
</script>
<a href="http://www.samspublishing.com/"
  target="mainWindow">Publisher</a><br />
<a href="http://www.amazon.com/gp/product/
➥0672328801" target="mainWindow">This book
➥at Amazon</a><br />
<a href="javascript:self.close();">Close window</a>
```

The Sitemap with the Close Link (sitemapwindow.html)

However, you should also close the sitemap from the
main window if another page is loaded there. In the
current example, loading any other page in the main
window redirects the browser off to another web

server; therefore, you can close the sitemap immediately. But before doing so, you should check whether the window is already closed, by taking a look at its closed property:

```
<script language="JavaScript"
  type="text/javascript">
var newwindow = window.open(
  "sitemapwindow.html",
  "sitemap",
  "width=320,height=100,directories=no,menubar=no,
➥toolbar=no,scrollbars=yes");
</script>
<body onunload="if (!newwindow.closed)
➥newwindow.close();"></body>
```

*Opening the Sitemap with the Auto-Closing Feature
(sitemapwindow.html)*

Checking for the Presence of a Pop-Up Blocker

```
var newwindow = window.open(
  "",
  "popupcheck",
  "width=100,height=100,directories=no,menubar=no,
➥toolbar=no");
```

Admittedly, all the previous phrases relied on the fact that the browser can open pop-ups. By default, most modern browsers allow pop-ups that are opened from the local server, but block pop-ups that are opened from the Internet. Also, various toolbars with their own pop-up blocking mechanism make the life of developers who rely on pop-ups harder.

The bad news first: There is no reliable way to ensure that pop-ups can *always* be opened. Some blockers support various levels of blocking, some of them allowing certain kinds of pop-ups, some of them disabling all pop-ups. Figure 9.5 shows a typical browser configuration screen.

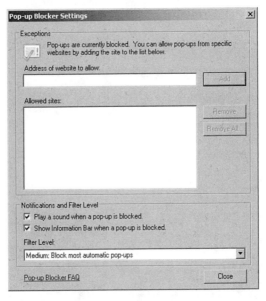

Figure 9.5 A pop-up blocker configuration.

The following code tries to detect whether a pop-up blocker is available: It opens a window and then checks whether it is there. If yes, it will be closed; otherwise, a pop-up blocker is most probably present:

```
<script language="JavaScript"
  type="text/javascript">
var newwindow = window.open(
  "",
  "popupcheck",
  "width=100,height=100,directories=no,menubar=no,
➥toolbar=no");
if (newwindow) {
  newwindow.close();
} else {
  window.alert("Pop-up blocker detected!");
}
</script>
```

Checking for a Pop-Up Blocker (popupcheck.html)

Figure 9.6 shows the result when a pop-up is blocked
(also visible from the notification bar on top of the
browser's content area).

Figure 9.6   A pop-up blocker has been detected.

TIP: The default behavior of most pop-up blockers is that
those pop-ups are allowed that are triggered by a user
action. So do not try to call window.open() when the

page has loaded, but rather call `window.open()` when the user clicks on something. But still you have no guarantee that the pop-up will actually appear.

Using JavaScript Frames

Working with frames from JavaScript is quite similar to working with the `window` object. Although frames miss some features a `window` object has, such as the `open()` method or ways to resize or reposition it, the basic properties of a frame are the same: The `document` property points to the `document` object that is loaded in the frame, and there are further properties like `location`.

The `frames` property of the main window (where the HTML document with the `<frameset>` element resides) is an array with all frames defined in that frameset. You can then access the frames either via their index (zero-based: `window.frames[0]`, `window.frames[1]`, ...) or via their `name` attribute: `window.frames["nameOfFrame"]`.

From every individual frame document (that is, documents that are loaded within a frame, even if they contain `<frameset>` elements as well), the frame structure can be accessed: `parent` references the document of the parent frame structure, whereas `top` jumps to the main document.

Changing the Contents of Two Frames at Once

```
top.frames[frame1].location.href = url1;
top.frames[frame2].location.href = url2;
```

One of the most common questions regarding JavaScript is how to change two frames at once. Although frames are becoming more and more unpopular among professional web developers, this question is still a hot topic.

Of course, JavaScript can come to the rescue. A function expects the names or indexes of the two frames, and of course the two URLs to load. Since the individual frames are changing during the course of the application, this function should be placed in the frameset document:

```
<script language="JavaScript"
  type="text/javascript">
function changeFrames(frame1, url1, frame2, url2) {
  top.frames[frame1].location.href = url1;
  top.frames[frame2].location.href = url2;
}
</script>
<frameset cols="150,*">
  <frame src="frame1a.html" name="navigation" />
  <frame src="frame2a.html" name="content" />
</frameset>
```

The Frameset with the JavaScript Function (frameset.html)

The left frame in this example is the navigation frame; the right frame is the content frame. When a link in the navigation frame is being clicked, both frames change, since every page in the right frame has an associated navigation page (with the current page highlighted) for the left frame.

```
Frame 1<br />
<a href="javascript:top.changeFrames('navigation',
➥'frame1b.html', 'content', 'frame2b.html');">
➥Frame 2</a>
```

The Frameset with the Navigation (frame1a.html)

A more general approach does not limit the number of frames to two, but just accepts an arbitrary number of frame names and URLs:

```
function changeFrames() {
  for (var i=0;
    i < Math.ceil(changeFrames.arguments.length/2);
    i++) {
    top.frames[changeFrames.arguments[2 * i]]
➥.location.href =
      changeFrames.arguments[2 * i + 1];
  }
}
```

*The Frameset with the More Flexible JavaScript Function
(frameset.html; excerpt)*

The file frameset.html in the download archive contains both versions of changeFrames(), with the less flexible one within a JavaScript comment.

TIP: Of course, this example works best if users without JavaScript are not excluded. So one approach would be to load a new page in the content frame, but use JavaScript to change the left frame as well, if the browser supports it:

```
<a href="frame2b" target="content"
  onclick="top.changeFrames('navigation',
    'frame1b.html', 'content', 'frame2b.html');
    return false;">Frame 2</a>
```

Using Hidden Frames for Data Storage

One quite convenient usage option for frames is to use hidden frames. This can, for instance, be used to store data across HTTP requests. Since all JavaScript data is lost if the page is unloaded, a hidden frame comes in handy to store data, for instance when creating a client-side shopping cart.

So all you have to do is create a frame with the height equal to one pixel or similar. Then, whenever you have to store away data, you just access the frame and save the required data in variables that are all accessible as properties of that frame:

```
top.frames["hiddenJsFrame"].variable = "value";
```

In a similar fashion, you can obviously also put common functions within that frame and then call them in a similar fashion:

```
top.frames["hiddenJsFrame"].functionName();
```

Using Iframes

```
window.frames["iframe1"].location.href =
  "iframe1b.html";
document.getElementById("iframe1").src =
  "iframe1b.html";
```

Iframes, or inline frames, are a very convenient way to create a section within a page that can be changed independently of the rest of the page. As the name already suggests, iframes are very similar to frames; however, some subtle changes exist. Here is the HTML markup for such an inline frame:

```
<iframe src="iframe1a.html" name="iframe1a"
  id="iframe1"></iframe>
```

Note that both a name and an ID are provided for the iframe, since there are two ways to approach the frame:

- Using the name and the `window.frames` array
- Using the ID and `document.getElementById()`

The former approach requires the `location.href` property to change the URL within the iframe; the latter approach returns an object that has an `src` property for that task:

- `window.frames["iframe1"].location.href = "iframe1b.html";`
- `document.getElementById("iframe1").src = "iframe1b.html";`

WARNING: Although iframes offer new capabilities for web applications, they also have their disadvantages. As you will see in Chapter 11, "AJAX (and Related Topics)," bookmarking and letting the back and forward buttons work as expected require some workaround—and these hacks work only when JavaScript is activated.

10

Web Services

Web Services are an amazing technology—on the server side. So what does this have to do with client-side JavaScript? Well, there is a way to call server-side scripts from the client side. Actually, there are two ways: one for Mozilla-based browsers, one for Internet Explorer. These two options are covered in this chapter; the next chapter then provides you with some interesting alternatives to the methods presented in this chapter.

Understanding Web Services

Some people say Web Services are just old wine in new bottles because the idea behind this is far from new. The basic principle is that two machines talk to each other. For instance, one machine contains some business logic or, more generally, some information, and the other machine requests this information (or wants to use the business logic).

This has been done for many years, but only a few years ago the major players sat together and started to work on protocols to put the whole communication on top of standards. Some of these standards are now under the aegis of the World Wide Web Consortium (W3C), whereas others are managed by the Organization for the Advancement of Structured Information Standards (OASIS) consortium.

A multitude of books are available on Web Services, with quite a lot of pages. However, in accordance with the concept of this phrasebook, this chapter keeps it simple but still gives you all you need to know. A protocol is used to transfer both the request to the Web Service and its response. There are several possibilities, but these three are the most common:

- XML-RPC stands for XML Remote Procedure Call. XML-RPC uses a simple XML dialect to transport function calls, parameters, and return values.

- REST stands for REpresentational State Transfer. REST basically uses HTTP requests (GET most of the time, but other HTTP verbs are also possible) as a Web Services call. The data returned via REST is plain XML.

- SOAP once stood for Simple Object Access Protocol, but because it is neither simple nor has too much to do with object access, today SOAP just stands for SOAP. It is a rather complex protocol but it overcomes many of the limitations of XML-RPC (which was, by the way, created by some parties who also worked on SOAP).

There are some fierce debates about which is better, this protocol or the next one. To make a short and ugly story short: All have advantages (and disadvantages).

Most of the time, REST or XML-RPC or SOAP calls are transported via HTTP as the carrier protocol. However, other protocols are also possible, including Simple Mail Transfer Protocol (SMTP) or even User Datagram Protocol (UDP).

There is one more important aspect regarding using SOAP. When you know exactly how a Web Service is implemented, you also know how to call (access, or consume) it. However, many times this information is not available, so there must be a kind of self-description of the Web Service that contains all relevant information, such as which methods or functions are exposed, which parameters and data types they expect, and what they return. This can be done using a specifically crafted XML file as well. The standard behind that is Web Services Description Language (WSDL). Today, WSDL is used for all relevant Web Services because it makes using Web Services quite simple. Most server-side technologies offer one (or more) means to just read in the WSDL and then access the Web Service like you would access a locally available class.

Using all this XML can become quite complicated. The next chapter covers XML as one of the aspects of the AJAX technology and gives you additional pointers. However, Mozilla browsers and Microsoft Internet Explorer feature their own way to access Web Services. This removes at least a bit of the complexity, but unfortunately it is not browser-agnostic.

Creating a Web Service with PHP

```
$soap = new SoapServer(
  'RandomNumberService.wsdl',
  array('uri' =>
    'http://javascript.phrasebook.org/')
);
```

So that the Web Service can be used, we first need one. The most popular server-side technology at the moment is PHP (PHP: Hypertext Preprocessor), so this is the obvious choice for implementing a Web Service. For this to work, you need a web server with PHP installed. Many affordable web hosting packages come with PHP nowadays, and PHP can also be installed on most types of web server. You can download the PHP distribution and source from its homepage, http://www.php.net/.

For this to work, you will need PHP 5 or later, and you have to enable the SOAP library that comes with it. On UNIX/Linux, you have to compile PHP with the configuration switch --enable-soap; users of Windows have to add the following line to the php.ini configuration file:

```
extension=php_soap.dll
```

Also, you need a WSDL file—that's a description for the Web Service, including which methods it exposes and which parameters it expects. The file RandomNumberService.wsdl contains all this information. Make sure that you look for the section <soap:address location="http://localhost/js/webservice.php" /> of the WSDL and adapt the URL to your local system.

Then, the following script implements a simple SOAP Web Service with one method (that returns a random number within a given interval):

```php
<?php
  $soap = new SoapServer(
    'RandomNumberService.wsdl',
    array('uri' =>
      'http://javascript.phrasebook.org/')
  );
  $soap->setClass('ServiceClass');
  $soap->handle();

  class ServiceClass {
    function randomNumber($lower, $upper) {
      return rand($lower, $upper);
    }
  }
?>
```

A PHP Web Service (webservice.php)

Creating a Web Service with ASP.NET

```
<%@ WebService language="C#"
  class="RandomNumberService" %>
```

One of the web technologies with the highest growth rate nowadays is ASP.NET from Microsoft. One of the nice features of the technology is that creating and using Web Services is a rather easy task.

To implement a Web Service, a file with the extension
.asmx must be created on the web server. Then, the
<%@ WebService %> directive must be on top of the
page. All methods that will be exposed as Web Services
methods must be prefixed with the [WebMethod] attribute. Here is a complete example:

```
<%@ WebService language="C#"
  class="RandomNumberService" %>

using System;
using System.Web.Services;

[WebService(Namespace=
➥"http://javascript.phrasebook.org/")]
public class RandomNumberService {

  [WebMethod]
  public int randomNumber(int lower, int upper) {
    Random r = new Random();
    return r.Next(lower, upper + 1);
  }
}
```

An ASP.NET Web Service (webservice.asmx)

When you call this page from an ASP.NET-enabled
web server in your web browser, you will get (depending on your configuration) a nice information page
that gives you some details about the service. If you
append ?WSDL to the URL, you get a WSDL description, automatically generated from ASP.NET.
Figure 10.1 shows how that looks.

Figure 10.1   The automatically generated detail
page for the ASP.NET Web Service.

Calling a Web Service from Internet Explorer

```
WebService.useService("webservice.php?WSDL",
  "RandomNumberService");
```

Some years ago, Microsoft provided a helper script to
access a Web Service from an HTML page using
JavaScript. For this to work, the Web Service must
reside on the same server as the JavaScript code.

Unfortunately, Microsoft stopped development of this
component and hid it deep in the Microsoft
Developers Network (MSDN). However, it is still
available and it works fine. Go to http://msdn.
microsoft.com/archive/en-us/samples/internet/
behaviors/library/webservice/default.asp, download
the file webservice.htc, and put the file in the
directory where your HTML file will reside (the
webservice.htc file is not part of the source code

download for this book). Then, the following markup loads the component:

```
<div id="WebService"
  style="behavior:url(webservice.htc);">
```

Then, WebService references the component and allows you to load a remote Web Service (useService() method), providing its WSDL description. The component then enables JavaScript code to call a web method (callService() method, providing a callback function, a method name, and parameters).

In the callback function, the result can be analyzed or just printed out, as the following sample code shows:

```
<html>
<head>
  <title>JavaScript</title>
  <script language="Javascript"
    type="text/javascript">
  function callWebService(f) {
    WebService.useService("webservice.php?WSDL",
      "RandomNumberService");
    WebService.RandomNumberService.callService(
      callbackFunction,
      "randomNumber",
      parseInt(f.elements["lower"].value),
      parseInt(f.elements["upper"].value));
  }

  function callbackFunction(result) {
    document.getElementById("random").innerHTML =
      result.value;
  }
  </script>
</head>
<body>
```

```
<div id="WebService"
  style="behavior:url(webservice.htc);">
</div>
<form>
  A number between
  <input type="text" name="lower" size="3"
    value="1" /> and
  <input type="text" name="upper" size="3"
    value="49" /> is
  <span id="random" /><br />
  <input type="button" value="Retrieve"
    onclick="callWebService(this.form);" />
</form>
</body>
</html>
```

Calling Web Services from Internet Explorer (webservice-ie-php.html)

Figure 10.2 shows the result: The random number comes from the Web Service on the web server.

NOTE: The preceding listing covers calling the PHP web service; the file `webservice-ie-aspnet.html` deals with the ASP.NET Web Service. The only change is that the name of the Web Service's URL has been changed; the rest of the code remains the same.

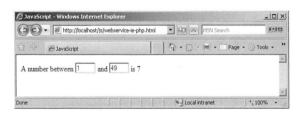

Figure 10.2   The random number comes from
the Web Service.

Calling a Web Service from a Mozilla Browser

```
var soapcall = new SOAPCall();
```

The Mozilla browsers support their own ways of calling Web Services. The JavaScript SOAPCall class can take care of creating the SOAP request. After instantiating the class, you have to set a couple of properties: the SOAP action (a SOAP header field, often the namespace of the Web Service plus the method name) and the absolute URI (including the name of the server) of the Web Service:

```
var soapcall = new SOAPCall();
soapcall.actionURI =
  "http://javascript.phrasebook.org/randomNumber";
soapcall.transportURI =
  "http://localhost/js/webservice.php";
```

Next, you create an array of all parameters you want to use in the Web Service call, by instantiating the SOAPParameter class:

```
var parameters = [
  new SOAPParameter(1, "lower"),
  new SOAPParameter(49, "upper")
];
```

Then, the encode() method prepares the Web Service call. The following parameters are expected:

- SOAP version (0 stands for SOAP 1.1 and is recommended)
- Name of the Web Service method to call
- Namespace of the Web Service

- Additional SOAP headers to send (as an array)
- Number of parameters to send
- Parameters to send (as an array)

The `asyncInvoke()` method actually calls the Web Service; you can provide a callback function that gets executed when the data comes back from the Web Service. This is an XML document, so you have to use the DOM to access the important information. The following code usually works:

```
function callbackFunction(result) {
  var returnData =
➡result.body.firstChild.firstChild.firstChild.data;
}
```

Here is the complete code:

```
<html>
<head>
  <title>JavaScript</title>
  <script language="Javascript"
    type="text/javascript">
  function callWebService(f) {
    var soapcall = new SOAPCall();
    soapcall.actionURI =
➡"http://javascript.phrasebook.org/randomNumber";
    soapcall.transportURI =
      "http://localhost/js/webservice.php";

    var parameters = [
      new SOAPParameter(parseInt(
        f.elements["lower"].value), "lower"),
      new SOAPParameter(parseInt(
        f.elements["upper"].value), "upper")
    ];
```

```
    soapcall.encode(
      0,
      "randomNumber",
      "http://javascript.phrasebook.org/",
      0,
      [],
      parameters.length,
      parameters
    );
    soapcall.asyncInvoke(callbackFunction);
  }

  function callbackFunction(result) {
    document.getElementById("random").innerHTML =
      result.body.firstChild.firstChild.firstChild
➡.data;
  }
  </script>
</head>
<body>
  <form>
    A number between
    <input type="text" name="lower" size="3"
      value="1" /> and
    <input type="text" name="upper" size="3"
      value="49" /> is
    <span id="random" /><br />
    <input type="button" value="Retrieve"
      onclick="callWebService(this.form);" />
  </form>
</body>
</html>
```

Calling a Web Service from Mozilla (webservice-mozilla-php.html)

NOTE: Again, do note that you may have to change the
URL for the Web Service call so that it fits your system.

Calling an ASP.NET Web Service from a Mozilla Browser

```
var schematype = schemacoll.getType(
  "integer",
  "http://www.w3.org/2001/XMLSchema"
);
```

There is one potential issue with the preceding code:
The data types for the parameters sent to the Web
Service are not provided. Unfortunately, some
Web Service implementations require this information
to work. Most notably, some .NET Web Services do
not work without this information.

It is hard to say who is to blame for that, Microsoft or
Mozilla, but at least there is a way to make these two
systems cooperate. To do so, you have to change the
way the parameters are created. After instantiating the
SOAPCall class, you have to load the correct encoding
for each parameter. In the example, the data type used
is integer, so that's what we are using. The parameters
array is now created in the following fashion:

```
var l = new SOAPParameter(parseInt(
  f.elements["lower"].value), "lower");
var u = new SOAPParameter(parseInt(
  f.elements["upper"].value), "upper");
var soapenc = new SOAPEncoding();
```

```
assenc = soapenc.getAssociatedEncoding(
  "http://schemas.xmlsoap.org/soap/encoding/",
  false
);
var schemacoll = assenc.schemaCollection;
var schematype = schemacoll.getType(
  "integer",
  "http://www.w3.org/2001/XMLSchema"
);
l.schemaType = schematype;
u.schemaType = schematype;
var parameters = [l, u];
```

Calling a Web Service with Distinctive Data Types from Mozilla
(webservice-mozilla-php.html; excerpt)

TIP: First, see whether the Web Service works without this
extra encoding. Older Mozilla versions do not support the
getAssociatedEncoding() method, whereas some newer
versions manage to cooperate with certain .NET Web
Services without the extra step of providing the data type.

11

AJAX (and Related Topics)

AJAX has generated a huge buzz since the term was coined in February 2005. And although there is a lot of (justified) criticism, regarding both the term and the technology mix it is promising, the whole hype around AJAX led to the rebirth of JavaScript. Not only are underestimated capabilities of JavaScript carried into the daily work of web developers, but more advanced JavaScript features also are en vogue again. This chapter presents not only the most important facts (and phrases) regarding JavaScript, but also related technologies, especially XML handling with JavaScript.

Understanding AJAX

Back in the 1990s, Microsoft added a new ActiveX object to its Internet Explorer web browser (version 5.0): XMLHttpRequest. This object was capable of sending HTTP requests to a server and evaluating the data returned from that, quite similar to the Web Services concept (but using another approach called REST—Representation State Transfer). This came by the request of the Outlook team that worked on the latest version of the web front-end for their software.

A few years later, this object was discovered by developers of the Mozilla project, and they decided to create their own version of XMLHttpRequest—of course, as a native JavaScript object, since ActiveX does not work cross-platform. Also, the Safari developers implemented XMLHttpRequest. Since the browser was based on the KHTML rendering engine of Konqueror, the code (donated by Apple) could also be applied to the KDE browser. Finally, the Opera and iCab browsers also added support for XMLHttpRequest.

While more and more web applications were using XMLHttpRequest, Jesse James Garrett wrote an article in February 2005 called "Ajax: A New Approach to Web Applications" (available online at http://www.adaptivepath.com/publications/essays/archives/000385.php). In this article, he coined the term "AJAX," which stands for "Asynchronous JavaScript + XML." He argued that his company was using XMLHttpRequest and JavaScript and DOM and XML and XSLT and XHTML and CSS, and it was getting more and more difficult to explain this to clients, especially if they were not technical people. Therefore, the term was invented, although this led to quite some criticism (for instance, no XML is required for AJAX). But still the coining of the term "AJAX" was the tipping point for the technology; from then on, it really took off.

From a technical point of view, AJAX is really all about using XMLHttpRequest to send HTTP requests to the web server (which must be in the same domain as the script, for security reasons) and using JavaScript to evaluate and display the data on the client. There is nothing more to it, but still there are even dedicated conferences for AJAX.

Initializing an AJAX Application

```
XMLHttp = new XMLHttpRequest();
XMLHttp = new ActiveXObject("Microsoft.XMLHTTP");
```

The basis of all AJAX applications is the aforementioned `XMLHttpRequest` object. All AJAX-enabled browsers support it natively, but in Internet Explorer the ActiveX object is required. There is one exception, though: Internet Explorer 7 comes with native `XMLHttpRequest` support. The best approach to create the object is to use `try...catch` and to instantiate the native object first (to get Internet Explorer 7 on the right track even though this browser still supports ActiveX), and then the ActiveX version:

```
if (window.XMLHttpRequest) {
  // instantiate native object
} else if (window.ActiveXObject) {
  // instantiate ActiveX object
}
```

Regarding the ActiveX object, there are several opportunities to instantiate it. The reason: Microsoft ships various versions of their XML library where this object is hidden. A bulletproof solution would be to check for all versions, using a convoluted piece of code. However, the following approach checks only the most important versions and works on Internet

Explorer 5 onward and on all other AJAX-aware browsers:

```javascript
function getXMLHttp() {
  var XMLHttp = null;
  if (window.XMLHttpRequest) {
    try {
      XMLHttp = new XMLHttpRequest();
    } catch (e) { }
  } else if (window.ActiveXObject) {
    try {
      XMLHttp = new ActiveXObject("Msxml2.XMLHTTP");
    } catch (e) {
      try {
        XMLHttp = new ActiveXObject(
          "Microsoft.XMLHTTP");
      } catch (e) { }
    }
  }
  return XMLHttp;
}
```

Creating the XMLHttpRequest Object (xmlhttp.js)

Sending a GET Request

```javascript
XMLHttp.open("GET", "phrasebook.txt");
XMLHttp.onreadystatechange = handlerFunction;
XMLHttp.send(null);
```

Sending an HTTP request to a server using XMLHttpRequest consists of the following steps:

1. Provide the URL and the HTTP verb to use.

2. Define a callback function when results arrive.

3. Send the request.

Step 1 can be taken with the open() method of the XMLHttpRequest object. This does not—unlike what the method name suggests—actually open an HTTP connection, but just initializes the object. You provide the HTTP verb to use (usually GET or POST) and the URL.

Step 2, the callback function, is provided to the onreadystatechange property of the object. Whenever the readyState property of XMLHttpRequest changes, this callback function is called. Finally, the send() method sends the HTTP request.

In the callback function, the readyState value 4 represents the state of the object we want: call completed. In that case, the responseText property contains the data returned from the server.

Here is a fully working example, sending a GET request to the server (a file called phrasebook.txt with simple text content) and evaluating the response of that call:

```
<script language="JavaScript"
  type="text/javascript" src="xmlhttp.js"></script>
<script language="JavaScript"
 type="text/javascript">
var XMLHttp = getXMLHttp();
XMLHttp.open("GET", "phrasebook.txt");
XMLHttp.onreadystatechange = handlerFunction;
XMLHttp.send(null);

function handlerFunction() {
  if (XMLHttp.readyState == 4) {
    window.alert("Returned data: " +
                 XMLHttp.responseText);
  }
}
</script>
```

Sending a GET Request (xmlhttpget.html)

Understating the States of XMLHttpRequest

All in all, the XMLHttpRequest object supports five states, as shown in Table 11.1. Depending on the implementation, up to all of these states happen during the execution of an AJAX script. That is the reason it is so important to always query the state before trying to access other XMLHttpRequest data.

Table 11.1   States of the XMLHttpRequest Object

State	Description
0	Uninitialized
1	Loading
2	Loaded
3	Waiting
4	Complete

Sending a POST Request

```
XMLHttp.setRequestHeader("Content-type",
  "application/x-www-form-urlencoded");
XMLHttp.send("word1=JavaScript&word2=Phrasebook");
```

When a GET request is being sent, all parameters are part of the URL. For POST, however, this data is sent in the body of the HTTP request. To do that with the XMLHttpRequest object, the parameters must be provided in the send() method. There is one caveat, though: If you want to access these parameters on the server side, the correct Content-type HTTP header must be set. This is done by using the setRequestHeader() method in the following fashion:

```
<script language="JavaScript"
  type="text/javascript" src="xmlhttp.js"></script>
<script language="JavaScript"
  type="text/javascript">
var XMLHttp = getXMLHttp();
XMLHttp.open("POST", "post.php");
XMLHttp.onreadystatechange = handlerFunction;
XMLHttp.setRequestHeader("Content-type",
  "application/x-www-form-urlencoded");
XMLHttp.send("word1=JavaScript&word2=Phrasebook");

function handlerFunction() {
  if (XMLHttp.readyState == 4) {
    window.alert("Returned data: " +
                 XMLHttp.responseText);
  }
}
</script>
```

Sending a POST Request (xmlhttppost.html)

The script posts to the URL post.php, which is a
simple PHP script just returning the data:

```
<?php
  if (isset($_POST['word1']) &&
      isset($_POST['word2'])) {
    echo $_POST['word1'] . ' ' . $_POST['word2'];
  } else {
    echo 'No data sent.';
  }
?>
```

The Target PHP Script of the POST Request (post.php)

Of course, you can provide any other script in any other server-side technology—or you just POST to a plain text file.

Sending a Synchronous Request

```
XMLHttp.open("GET", "phrasebook.txt", false);
```

By default, HTTP requests via XMLHttpRequest are asynchronous, which explains the need for a callback function. However, when you set the third parameter of the open() method to false, the request is a synchronous one, which means that the script execution is stopped until data comes back from the server. The following code makes use of that:

```
<script language="JavaScript"
  type="text/javascript" src="xmlhttp.js"></script>
<script language="JavaScript"
  type="text/javascript">
window.onload = function() {
  var XMLHttp = getXMLHttp();
  XMLHttp.open("GET", "phrasebook.txt", false);
  XMLHttp.send(null);
  document.getElementById("output").innerHTML =
    "Returned data: " + XMLHttp.responseText;
}
</script>
<p id="output">Calling the server ...</p>
```

Sending a Synchronous Request (xmlhttpsync.html)

Note that the whole code is executed only after the full page has been loaded; otherwise, the access to the output HTML element may fail.

WARNING: Synchronous calls may be convenient, but from a usability and performance point of view, they should be avoided. The script execution stops completely while the call is made, which could turn into a real nightmare with slow connections or servers under a heavy load.

Receiving Multiple Data from the Server

```
var data = XMLHttp.responseText.split("\n");
```

By default, the responseText property exists only once, so the whole data returned from the server will be put into the string. However, often it is required that more than one piece of data is returned from the XMLHttpRequest call. There are several solutions for this scenario, but probably the easiest one is to return multiple data and separate the individual data using a separation character that does not occur in the data itself (for instance, a tabulator or a new line or the pipe symbol). Then it is possible to use JavaScript to access this information.

For this phrase, the following server-side text file is queried using HTTP. (In a real-world scenario, there would certainly be a dynamic script on the server side, but for demonstration purposes, the static file is just good enough.)

```
JavaScript
Phrasebook
Sams Publishing
```

Multiple Data in One File (phrasebook-multiple.txt)

Then, the following code accesses the individual information in the returned data; Figure 11.1 shows the result.

```
<script language="JavaScript"
  type="text/javascript" src="xmlhttp.js"></script>
<script language="JavaScript"
  type="text/javascript">
var XMLHttp = getXMLHttp();
XMLHttp.open("GET", "phrasebook-multiple.txt");
XMLHttp.onreadystatechange = handlerFunction;
XMLHttp.send(null);

function handlerFunction() {
  if (XMLHttp.readyState == 4) {
    var data = XMLHttp.responseText.split("\n");
    window.alert(data[0] + " " + data[1] +
                " by " + data[2]);
  }
}
</script>
```

Working with Multiple Data from the Server (xmlhttpmultiple.html)

Figure 11.1   The server sends multiple data.

Aborting an HTTP Request

```
XMLHttp.abort();
```

Depending on the browser, only a limited number of HTTP requests can be done at a time. Especially if you have a page with multiple AJAX components (the modern term for this is "mashup"), you may run into trouble. Therefore, aborting an HTTP request may become a necessity.

The method used for that is abort(). The following code aborts the request if it has not been fully executed after five seconds. To demonstrate this behavior, the PHP script delay.php that is called by the code takes 10 seconds to execute. Also note that the readyState property is checked first: if it is 0 or 4, there is nothing to abort.

```
<script language="JavaScript"
  type="text/javascript" src="xmlhttp.js"></script>
<script language="JavaScript"
  type="text/javascript">
var XMLHttp = getXMLHttp();
```

```
XMLHttp.open("GET", "delay.php?" + Math.random());
XMLHttp.onreadystatechange = handlerFunction;
XMLHttp.send(null);
window.setTimeout("timeout();", 5000);

function handlerFunction() {
  if (XMLHttp.readyState == 4) {
    window.alert("Returned data: " +
                 XMLHttp.responseText);
  }
}

function timeout() {
  if (XMLHttp.readyState != 4 &&
      XMLHttp.readyState != 0) {
    XMLHttp.onreadystatechange = function() { };
    XMLHttp.abort();
    window.alert("Request aborted");
  }
}
</script>
```

Aborting an HTTP Request (xmlhttpabort.html)

Five seconds after loading this page, the request is
aborted.

TIP: Appending the result of Math.random() to the URL
to call causes caching for the script delay.php to be
disabled, since the URL is a different one every time.

Retrieving HTTP Headers

```
var headers = XMLHttp.getAllResponseHeaders();
```

The method getAllResponseHeaders() (see preceding code) returns all HTTP headers in the HTTP response, whereas the getResponseHeader() method returns just one specific header. The following code shows how to get information about the type of web server used:

```
<script language="JavaScript"
  type="text/javascript" src="xmlhttp.js"></script>
<script language="JavaScript"
  type="text/javascript">
var XMLHttp = getXMLHttp();
XMLHttp.open("GET", "phrasebook.txt");
XMLHttp.onreadystatechange = handlerFunction;
XMLHttp.send(null);

function handlerFunction() {
  if (XMLHttp.readyState == 4) {
    var servertype =
      XMLHttp.getResponseHeader("Server");
    window.alert("Web server used: " + servertype);
  }
}
</script>
```

Retrieving an HTTP Response Header (responseheader.html)

Note that not all servers send this header; some also put fake data in it to make server profiling harder.

Receiving XML from the Server

```
var xml = XMLHttp.responseXML;
```

The responseText property works well for a limited amount of unstructured data. However, a more elegant approach for using complex, structured data within an AJAX application promises to be the responseXML property. When accessing this property, you get the response of the HTTP request as a JavaScript XML DOM object—of course, only if the server returns valid XML; otherwise, you get null.

Accessing the details of the XML object is quite similar to accessing DOM elements from JavaScript. For this phrase, the following sample XML file will be used:

```
<books>
  <book pubdate="2006">
    <title>JavaScript Phrasebook</title>
    <publisher>Sams Publishing</publisher>
  <book>
</books>
```

Sample XML Data (phrasebook.xml)

For the web browsers to read in this XML (Internet Explorer especially is very strict in that regard), the correct MIME type must be sent to the client: text/xml. If you are using Apache, the following configuration in mime.types should do the trick, but is already there by default:

```
text/xml
```

On Internet Information Services, you can configure the MIME types in the administration console (Start, Run, inetmgr). Alternatively, let a server-side script serve the file with the correct MIME type; generally this is a must if you are using server-side technology to generate the XML:

```php
<?php
  header('Content-type: text/xml');
  readfile('phrasebook.xml');
?>
```

Setting the Correct Response MIME Type (phrasebook.xml.php)

Then, the following code accesses the information in the XML file, using the DOM structure and methods like getElementsByTagName() and getAttribute(). Figure 11.2 shows the result.

```javascript
<script language="JavaScript"
  type="text/javascript" src="xmlhttp.js"></script>
<script language="JavaScript"
  type="text/javascript">
var XMLHttp = getXMLHttp();
XMLHttp.open("GET", "phrasebook.xml");
XMLHttp.onreadystatechange = handlerFunction;
XMLHttp.send(null);

function handlerFunction() {
  if (XMLHttp.readyState == 4) {
    var xml = XMLHttp.responseXML;
    var book = xml.getElementsByTagName("book")[0];
    var pubdate = book.getAttribute("pubdate");
    var title, publisher;
    for (var i=0; i<book.childNodes.length; i++) {
```

```
      if (book.childNodes[i].nodeName == "title") {
        title = book.childNodes[i].firstChild
➥.nodeValue;
      } else if (book.childNodes[i].nodeName ==
➥"publisher") {
        publisher = book.childNodes[i].firstChild
➥.nodeValue;
      }
   }
   window.alert(title + " by " + publisher +
               " (" + pubdate + ")");
  }
}
</script>
```

Extracting Information from the HTTP Response (xmlhttpxml.html)

Figure 11.2   The data from the XML file.

TIP: Another useful property of the XML DOM document is documentElement, which is a shortcut to the root element of the XML data. So if the root node contains attributes you are interested in (as some Web Services do), documentElement comes in handy.

Understanding JSON

JSON is, just like AJAX, rather a term than a technology. However, unlike AJAX, JSON also has its own homepage, http://www.json.org/.

JSON, which stands for JavaScript Object Notation, is a longtime neglected and underestimated feature of JavaScript—a quite compact notation for arrays and objects. A lot of books define JavaScript arrays in the following way, for instance:

```
var ajax = new Array(
  "Asynchronous", "JavaScript", "+", "XML");
```

However, there is a more compact way, using square brackets:

```
var ajax = [
  "Asynchronous", "JavaScript", "+", "XML"];
```

The same thing goes for objects (which are more or less elevated arrays in JavaScript), this time using curly braces. The following code defines an object with three properties:

```
var book = {
  "title": "JavaScript Phrasebook",
  "publisher": "Sams Publishing",
  "pubdate": 2006
};
```

Both "shortcuts" can be combined together to represent complex data as a string. And that is what JSON is all about: Since it can be quite nicely expressed in a string, it is a great data serialization format. It is rather trivial to create a JSON representation of an object on the server side, and it is even simpler to convert this string to a JavaScript object on the client side, as the next phrase shows.

Using JSON for Data (De)Serialization

```
var json = XMLHttp.responseText;
var book = eval("(" + json + ")");;
```

JSON is becoming more and more the de facto standard data exchange format for AJAX applications. Many AJAX frameworks support JSON, many Web Services provide a JSON interface, and PHP 6 will most probably feature JSON support at the core of the language.

Using JSON within JavaScript is quite simple, as well. The preceding code evaluates JSON and converts it into a JavaScript object—a simple eval() function call does the trick.

The JSON notation from the previous sidebar, "Understanding JSON," is stored in a file called phrasebook.json; then, the following code reads in this file using XMLHttpRequest and then outputs some data from it:

```
<script language="JavaScript"
  type="text/javascript" src="xmlhttp.js"></script>
<script language="JavaScript"
  type="text/javascript">
var XMLHttp = getXMLHttp();
XMLHttp.open("GET", "phrasebook.json");
XMLHttp.onreadystatechange = handlerFunction;
XMLHttp.send(null);

function handlerFunction() {
  if (XMLHttp.readyState == 4) {
    var json = XMLHttp.responseText;
```

```
    var book = eval("(" + json + ")");
    var pubdate = book.pubdate;
    var title = book.title;
    var publisher = book.publisher;
    window.alert(title + " by " + publisher +
                " (" + pubdate + ")");
  }
}
</script>
```

Using JSON for Data Deserialization (xmlhttpjson.html)

WARNING: Using eval() is generally a bad idea, since you introduce a serious security vulnerability if the JSON comes from a nontrustworthy source. Due to the same-domain restriction of XMLHttpRequest, the JSON code can usually be trusted, but if you want to feel safer, download the JSON library json.js from http://www.json.org/js.html. Then, the following code replaces the eval() call:

var book = json.parseJSON();

Creating a Waiting Screen

```
document.getElementById("loading").style.visibility
➡= "hidden";
```

One of the largest obstacles for modern web applications is latency: Something happens, but in the background. You do have to inform the users; otherwise, they will not notice that something is coming up. One way of doing this is by changing the mouse cursor (see Chapter 4, "CSS"); another way is by using a waiting banner. Many applications let a banner labeled with "waiting" or "loading" fade in when an XMLHttpRequest call is executed; one of the first websites to use this was Google Mail.

Actually, this phrase requires more DHTML than AJAX. When the (asynchronous!) call is sent to the server, the loading screen is shown and positioned in the upper-right corner (you can, of course, use any arbitrary position of your liking). After data comes back from the server, the banner is made invisible again. The following code implements this in a browser-agnostic fashion:

```
<script language="JavaScript"
  type="text/javascript" src="xmlhttp.js"></script>
<script language="JavaScript"
  type="text/javascript">
var XMLHttp = getXMLHttp();
window.onload = function() {
  XMLHttp.open("GET", "delay.php?" + Math.random());
  XMLHttp.onreadystatechange = handlerFunction;
  XMLHttp.send(null);
  with (document.getElementById("loading")) {
    style.visibility = "visible";
    if (navigator.appName ==
      "Microsoft Internet Explorer") {
      style.posLeft =
        document.body.clientWidth - 75;
      style.posTop = 0;
    } else {
      style.left = (window.innerWidth - 75) + "px";
      style.top = "0px";
    }
  }
}
```

```
function handlerFunction() {
  if (XMLHttp.readyState == 4) {
    document.getElementById("loading").style
➥.visibility = "hidden";
    window.alert("Returned data: " +
                 XMLHttp.responseText);
  }
}
</script>
<span id="loading" style="position: absolute;
➥visibility: hidden; background-color: red;
➥width: 75px;">Loading ...</span>
```

Implementing a Waiting Screen (waiting.html)

Figure 11.3 shows the browser while waiting for results: The banner appears (and vanishes again after the data from the HTTP request has arrived).

Figure 11.3   The waiting screen.

WARNING: The XMLHttpRequest object will not notice you if anything with your HTTP request goes wrong, which also includes timeouts. So you should use the pattern shown in the phrase "Aborting an HTTP Request" to check the status of the request after a certain period. If the request has not been completed until then, you should restart it—or print out an error message, and let the waiting banner disappear.

Solving the Bookmark Problem

```
var data = unescape(location.hash.substring(1));
```

One of the main issues with AJAX applications today is that it is not possible to bookmark a page. Since the contents of a page can change thanks to XMLHttpRequest calls, but the URL stays the same, bookmarking does not work.

There is, however, a workaround. Caveat: This workaround is just the shell of the code you have to write; the actual work you have to do (depending on your application) is how to persist data and then apply it back to the page.

The trick is to append data that identifies the current state of the page to the URL. Not in the form of a GET parameter (since this would cause a reload of the page), but in the hash:

```
http://server/file.html#info
```

The data denoted here with info must identify the current page status. The implementation details largely depend on how AJAX is used on the page.

Whenever the current state of the page changes, the page's hash (location.hash in JavaScript) must be updated. Then, the following code snippet reads in this information after the page is loaded. You have to implement the applyData() function that takes care of transforming the information in location.hash into actual content on the page.

```
window.onload = function() {
  if (location.hash.length >= 2) {
    var data = unescape(location.hash.substring(1));
```

```
    applyData(data);
  }
};
```

This, of course, increases the amount of work to be done, but your users benefit greatly from this convenient feature. Unfortunately, this approach does not work (yet) with Safari and Konqueror since they handle `location.hash` in a different way.

WARNING: Do not try to just put JSON into the hash and then call `eval()`; otherwise, an attacker could just put malicious JavaScript code in the URL that is then run in the context of your site. This kind of attack is called Cross-Site Scripting (XSS) and is very dangerous. Therefore, always validate data before using it.

Solving the Back Button Problem

```
window.frames["loader"].window.location.search =
  "?" + escape(data);
```

A problem related to the issue tackled in the previous phrase is the back button (and, of course, the forward button as well). When the page's URL does not change but its contents do, the back button does not really work as expected.

To solve this problem—and again this phrase can show only a generic approach, not a full solution, since there are so many implementation-dependent details—two subproblems have to be worked on:

- First, you have to make sure that upon loading of a page, the information in `location.hash` is applied to the page (if you use the previous phrase, this work has already been done).

- Second, you have to make sure that the various pages with the new hash are in the browser's history; otherwise, the back and forward buttons will not work. This is done automatically with Mozilla browsers, but not with Internet Explorer.

The solution to the second subproblem is to use a hidden iframe that will load an invisible page, just to get an entry in the history of the page. Here is the iframe:

```
<iframe src="loader.html" name="loader"
  style="display:none"></iframe>
```

Whenever something happens on the page (AJAX-wise), the loader frame must be forced to load again, with data appended to the URL (unlike the previous code, this time there *must* be a reload):

```
if (window.ActiveXObject) {
  window.frames["loader"].window.location.search =
    "?" + escape(data);
}
```

Finally, the loader frame must take care of applying any loaded data to the main document; at least for Internet Explorer this is required, since in this browser the back and forward buttons change the contents of the iframe!

```
window.onload = function() {
  if (location.search.length >= 2) {
    var data = unescape(
      location.search.substring(1));
    top.applyData(data);
  }
};
```

This makes the coder's life much more complicated, especially if there are many different AJAX effects on the page. But just to repeat one of the final sentences from the previous phrase: Your users benefit greatly from this convenient feature. And again, this work-around does not work with Safari and Konqueror (yet).

Understanding XSLT

In 1999, the W3C published the XSLT 1.0 specification. The acronym stands for Extensible Stylesheet Language Transformations. This is a language based on XML to transform data into another form. Most of the time, the output data is HTML, but other formats are also possible. On the Web, however, usually HTML is the way to go.

XSLT works with templates; within these templates you can, among other things, access node values and also attribute values in the XML source file. The following code shows a sample XSLT file:

```
<?xml version="1.0" encoding="UTF-8" ?>
<xsl:stylesheet version="1.0"
  xmlns:xsl="http://www.w3.org/1999/XSL/Transform">
<xsl:template match="/">
<ul>
  <xsl:for-each select="books/book">
    <li>
      <xsl:value-of select="title" />
      by
      <xsl:value-of select="publisher" />
      (<xsl:value-of select="@pubdate" />)
    </li>
  </xsl:for-each>
```

```
</ul>
</xsl:template>
</xsl:stylesheet>
```

The XSLT File (phrasebooks.xsl)

Using XSLT

```
var process = new XSLTProcessor();
```

Both Internet Explorer and Mozilla browsers do support XSLT from JavaScript. However, the approach is very different. For Microsoft Internet Explorer, once again ActiveX is required (also with Internet Explorer 7). You first load the XSLT file, then the XML (coming from XMLHttpRequest, of course). Finally, the result of the XSL transformation is available as a string and can, for instance, be appended to the page.

Mozilla browsers, on the other hand, use a different approach; they rely exclusively on native object. The result, however, is different from the Internet Explorer implementation. At the end, you get a DOM fragment, which you can append to the current page's DOM.

The following code covers both major browser types:

```
<script language="JavaScript"
  type="text/javascript" src="xmlhttp.js"></script>
<script language="JavaScript"
  type="text/javascript">
var XMLHttp = getXMLHttp();
window.onload = function() {
  XMLHttp.open("GET", "phrasebooks.xml");
  XMLHttp.onreadystatechange = handlerFunction;
```

```
  XMLHttp.send(null);
}

function handlerFunction() {
  if (XMLHttp.readyState == 4) {
    var xml = XMLHttp.responseXML;
    if (window.ActiveXObject) {
      var xslt = new ActiveXObject(
        "MSXML2.FreeThreadedDOMDocument");
      xslt.async = false;
      xslt.load("phrasebooks.xsl");
      var template = new ActiveXObject(
        "MSXML2.XSLTemplate");
      template.stylesheet = xslt;
      var process = template.createProcessor();
      process.input = xml;
      process.transform();
      var para = document.createElement("p");
      para.innerHTML = process.output;
      document.body.appendChild(para);
    } else if (window.XSLTProcessor) {
      var xslt = document.implementation
➥.createDocument("", "", null);
      xslt.async = false;
      xslt.load("phrasebooks.xsl");
      var process = new XSLTProcessor();
      process.importStylesheet(xslt);
      var result = process.transformToFragment(
        xml, document);
      document.body.appendChild(result);
    }
  }
}
</script>
```

Using XSLT with JavaScript (xmlhttpxsl.html)

Figure 11.4 shows the output of the transformation: The data in the XML file is presented as a bulleted list.

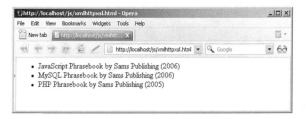

Figure 11.4   The outcome of the XSL transformation.

As Figure 11.4 also demonstrates, the Opera browser (from version 9 onward) has a compatible XSLT implementation, using the Mozilla approach.

Using an XML Library

```
var result = xsltProcess(xml, xslt);
```

As you can see, using XSLT from JavaScript can be quite tricky if it is to work on as many browsers as possible. In this case, using an external framework can really save a lot of time and effort.

Google has created such a framework ("AJAXSLT") which is available free (under a BSD license) at http://goog-ajaxslt.sourceforge.net/. The following phrase uses version 0.4 of the framework, which you can also see from the paths used in the code. The framework itself is also not part of the source code downloads for this book.

The following phrase does the XSLT transformation, but this time relies on the functionality offered by AJAXSLT.

```
<script language="JavaScript"
  type="text/javascript" src="xmlhttp.js"></script>
<script src="ajaxslt-0.4/misc.js"
  type="text/javascript"></script>
<script src="ajaxslt-0.4/dom.js"
  type="text/javascript"></script>
<script src="ajaxslt-0.4/xpath.js"
  type="text/javascript"></script>
<script src="ajaxslt-0.4/xslt.js"
  type="text/javascript"></script>
<script language="JavaScript"
  type="text/javascript">
var xml = null;
var xslt = null;
var XMLHttp1 = getXMLHttp();
var XMLHttp2 = getXMLHttp();
window.onload = function() {
  XMLHttp1.open("GET", "phrasebooks.xml");
  XMLHttp1.onreadystatechange = handlerFunction1;
  XMLHttp1.send(null);
  XMLHttp2.open("GET", "phrasebooks.xsl");
  XMLHttp2.onreadystatechange = handlerFunction2;
  XMLHttp2.send(null);
}

function handlerFunction1() {
  if (XMLHttp1.readyState == 4) {
    xml = xmlParse(XMLHttp1.responseText);
    if (xslt != null) {
      transform();
    }
```

```
  }
}

function handlerFunction2() {
  if (XMLHttp2.readyState == 4) {
    xslt = xmlParse(XMLHttp2.responseText);
    if (xml != null) {
      transform();
    }
  }
}

function transform() {
  var result = xsltProcess(xml, xslt);
  document.getElementById("output").innerHTML =
    result;
}
</script>
<div id="output"></div>
```

Using XSLT with JavaScript and AJAXSLT (ajaxslt.html)

This not only works fine (as you can see, most of the code is "spent" for loading the XML and XSL files), but also works cross-browser, as Figure 11.5 (shot in Konqueror) demonstrates. Another nice feature: You can also use XPath with this library. Both Internet Explorer and Mozilla browsers and Opera work with XPath, but in an even more incompatible way than they do regarding XSLT. Also, the AJAXSLT XPath support can deal with other browsers, as well.

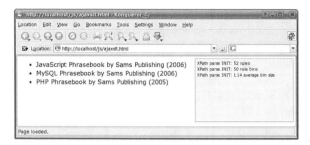

Figure 11.5 With AJAXLST the transformation
even works in Konqueror.

Using the Yahoo! Web Service

```
<script language="JavaScript" type="text/javascript"
  src="http://api.search.yahoo.com/WebSearchService/
V1/webSearch?appid=XXXXX&query=JavaScript&output=
json&callback=showResults">
</script>
```

More and more Web Services provide a JSON interface, and among the first ones to do so were the
Yahoo! Web Services. After a (free) registration at
http://api.search.yahoo.com/webservices/register_
application, you get your personal application ID. This
ID is tied to your application and must be used instead
of the *XXXXX* placeholder in this phrase. Then, the preceding <script> tag not only calls the Web Service and
expects JSON back, but also provides the name of a
callback function that is called after the data is there.
So your application receives JavaScript code from the
Yahoo! server and executes it—which means you have
to trust Yahoo! in order to use it. Then, the callback
function gets a JavaScript object with the Yahoo!
search results.

The following code then creates a bulleted list with
the data from the Web Service. More information
about the specific format of the data returned from
Yahoo! can be found at the online documentation
at http://developer.yahoo.com/search/web/V1/
webSearch.html. Figure 11.6 shows the output of
this code.

```
<script language="JavaScript"
  type="text/javascript">
function showResults(data) {
  var ul = document.getElementById("output");
  for (var i=0; i < data.ResultSet.Result.length;
➥i++) {
    var text = document.createTextNode(
      data.ResultSet.Result[i].Title + " - " +
      data.ResultSet.Result[i].Url);
    var li = document.createElement("li");
    li.appendChild(text);
    ul.appendChild(li);
  }
}
</script>
<body>
  <p><ul id="output"></ul></p>
</body>
<script language="JavaScript" type="text/javascript"
  src="http://api.search.yahoo.com/WebSearchService/
➥V1/webSearch?appid=XXXXX&query=JavaScript&
➥output=json&callback=showResults">
</script>
```

Calling the Yahoo! Web Service with JavaScript
(yahoowebservice.html)

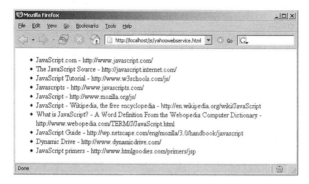

Figure 11.6   The Yahoo! search results.

Using an AJAX Framework

The more AJAX you are using on your website, the more you should look into available AJAX frameworks that can facilitate working with XMLHttpRequest and other advanced JavaScript features.

Which framework to choose depends largely on the server-side technology that is used. There are several AJAX frameworks for both Java (for example, Zimbra, at http://www.zimbra.com/) and ASP.NET 2.0 (for example, Atlas, at http://atlas.asp.net/); PHP knows too many frameworks to mention (including the PEAR package at http://pear.php.net/package/HTML_AJAX).

Quite interesting are also technology-independent AJAX frameworks that rather focus on the JavaScript side of things. Dojo, especially (http://www.dojo-toolkit.org/), is worth mentioning, since it offers workarounds similar to those mentioned in this chapter to make the back and forward buttons work again.

One of the oldest frameworks, by the way, is considered to be Tibet (http://www.technicalpursuit.com/), which started being worked on (at least conceptually) in 1997 and saw its first release in 1999.

So choose your framework wisely depending on the server-side technology—are you exclusively using one server technology, or are you more customer driven? Depending on this information, the features of the various frameworks, and especially the development activity (since many projects never really get off the ground or stall after some months), you pick a framework; but quite often the phrases in this chapter will give you all you need to turn your web application into an AJAX application.

12

Embedded Media

HTML and JavaScript are a killer combination, but sometimes more is required to create a modern web application. Therefore, HTML enables web developers to integrate other content in a site; generally, you need a browser plug-in for that. This chapter shows how to access this content and gives a few pointers for the most widely used content types. Note that most phrases in this chapter do not come with code downloads.

Accessing Embedded Media

document.media

The "official" HTML element to embed media is `<object>`. However, to have a cross-browser site, usually an `<embed>` object is embedded within the `<object>` element. To make accessing the embedded object as easy as possible, the `<object>` element's id attribute should match the `<embed>` object's name attribute:

```
<object classid="..." id="media">
  <embed name="media"></embed>
</object>
```

Then, you can access the embedded media using the shortcut from the beginning of this phrase. Of course, you could also use `document.getElementById()` to access the `<object>` element; all `<embed>` elements reside in the `document.embeds` array. As you can see, the shortcut is much more convenient here.

Checking for Plug-Ins

```
if (new ActiveXObject(
    "ShockwaveFlash.ShockwaveFlash.8")) { }
```

In Mozilla browsers, the `about:plugins` special URL provides a list of all available plug-ins, as Figure 12.1 shows; this works in Opera as well.

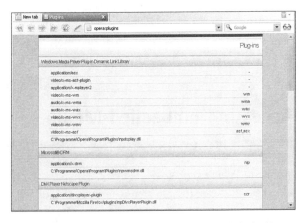

Figure 12.1 Opera shows a list of all installed plugins.

Depending on the chosen browser, there are two ways to actively check for the presence of a certain plug-in:

- On Mozilla browsers and Opera (which uses the same API), `navigator.plugins` is an array with all plug-ins. Every array element exposes the name, filename, and description of every plug-in. Also, `navigator.mimeTypes` contains a list of all supported MIME types the plug-in can support.

- On Internet Explorer (Windows only), you can try to instantiate the associated class the plug-in exposes, by using the `ActiveXObject` constructor.

The following code tries to detect the Flash plug-in. For Internet Explorer, the name of the associated COM object is used; for other browsers, the code is looking for a plug-in called "Shockwave Flash."

```
<script language="JavaScript"
type="text/javascript">
var hasFlash = false;
if (window.ActiveXObject) {
  try {
    if (new ActiveXObject(
      "ShockwaveFlash.ShockwaveFlash.8")) {
      hasFlash = true;
    }
  } catch (e) {
  }
} else if (navigator.plugins) {
  if (navigator.plugins["Shockwave Flash"]) {
      hasFlash = true;
  }
}
window.alert(hasFlash);
</script>
```

Detecting the Flash Plug-In (plugin.html)

> **WARNING:** The array `navigator.plugins` is also available on Internet Explorer, but empty. Therefore, you have to first check for `window.ActiveXObject`, then for `navigator.plugins`. It will not work the other way around.

Coping with Recent Internet Explorer Versions

A court ruling forced Microsoft to release an update for its browser in March and April 2006 that changed the behavior of embedded media. Without the user "activating" the embedded data by clicking on it, many events are not fired and other restrictions apply. Figure 12.2 shows the information the browser provides in that case.

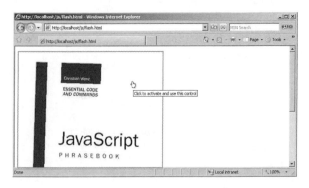

Figure 12.2   The embedded media (here: a Flash movie) is inactive.

However, on http://msdn.microsoft.com/workshop/author/dhtml/overview/activating_activex.asp,

Microsoft explains a workaround. The idea is to use JavaScript to include the `<object>` element on the page. Yet due to the technical details of the ruling, the JavaScript code that creates (via the `document.write()` method) the `<object>` element must reside in an external file. So what you want to do is to first use a `<script>` element in the following fashion:

```
<script language="JavaScript"
  type="text/javascript" src="externalFile.js">
</script>
```

Then, in the `externalFile.js` file, you output the markup that loads the embedded media file:

```
document.write("<object classid=\"...\"
...></object>");
```

TIP: Of course, the embedded media then works only when JavaScript is activated, so you should also have a solution in an `<noscript>` element. Due to the software patent that caused the court ruling, it is also possible that other browser vendors may have to implement a similar new behavior for embedded media.

Accessing Multimedia Content

Accessing multimedia content (audio or video data) in the browser is quite difficult. There are a lot of plug-ins, and every version seems to change something in respect to its predecessor. So for up-to-date or version-specific information regarding accessing the various plug-ins, the vendor's website is the best choice.

However, there's some good news as well. The major plug-ins for multimedia data, currently Windows

Media Player, Real Player, and Apple QuickTime, are quite similar with regard to method names. So after you've accessed the plug-in as described at the beginning of this chapter, the methods from Table 12.1 provide you with the essential functionality you need for working with the embedded media.

Table 12.1   Methods for Multimedia Functionality

Action	Windows Media Player	Real Player	QuickTime
Play	play()	DoPlay()	play()
Stop	stop()	DoStop()	stop()
Pause	pause()	DoPause()	pause()
Volume	volume	GetVolume()/ SetVolume()	GetVolume()/ SetVolume()

Accessing Java Content

```
document.JavaApplet.setString(field.value);
```

Java was once thought to be the dominant web format, but nowadays it works more in the background than in the front-end. However, you still see some Java applets embedded in web pages from time to time, although the Java plug-in lacks the large penetration of the Flash plug-in.

When a Java applet is embedded in a page, you can call all public methods of this applet. The following, very simple applet exposes its setString() method, which sets a private variable and then repaints the applet:

```
import java.applet.*;
import java.awt.*;

public class JavaApplet extends Applet
{
  private String _s = "Welcome!";

  public void paint(Graphics g) {
    g.setColor(Color.black);
    g.drawString(_s, 20, 20);
  }

  public void setString(String s) {
    this._s = s;
    this.repaint();
  }
}
```

A Simple Java Applet (JavaApplet.java)

After this applet is compiled into a class, the following JavaScript code calls the `setString()` method whenever the content of the text field changes. Figure 12.3 shows the result.

```
<script language="JavaScript"
  type="text/javascript">
function paint(field) {
  document.JavaApplet.setString(field.value);
}
</script>
<applet code="JavaApplet.class" name="JavaApplet"
  width="150" height="75"></applet><br />
<input type="text" onkeyup="paint(this);" />
```

Accessing Java with JavaScript (java.html)

Figure 12.3   The applet changes while
you are typing.

Accessing Flash Content

```
document.flash.Play();
document.flash.Rewind();
document.flash.StopPlay();
```

Flash movies can also be controlled via JavaScript.
Among other things, you can start, stop, and pause the
movie. For these purposes, the plug-in exposes the
Play(), Rewind(), and StopPlay() methods. The follow-
ing listing implements a simple control station for the
Flash movie:

```
<object
  classid="clsid:d27cdb6e-ae6d-11cf-96b8-
444553540000"
  codebase="http://fpdownload.macromedia.com/pub/
    ➥shockwave/cabs/flash/swflash.cab
    ➥#version=7,0,0,0"
  width="400" height="550" id="flash">
  <param name="allowScriptAccess"
    value="sameDomain" />
```

```
  <param name="movie" value="flash.swf" />
  <embed src="flash.swf" width="400" height="550"
    name="flash"
    allowScriptAccess="sameDomain"
    type="application/x-shockwave-flash"
    pluginspage="http://www.macromedia.com/go/
    ➥getflashplayer" />
</object>
<a href="javascript:document.flash.Play();">
    Play</a>
<a href="javascript:document.flash.Rewind();">
    Stop</a>
<a href="javascript:document.flash.StopPlay();">
    Pause</a>
```

Accessing a Flash Movie from JavaScript (flash.html)

NOTE: The allowScriptAccess options set in both the
<object> and the <embed> elements allow JavaScript to
actually access the Flash movie.

Index

How can we make this index more useful? Email us at indexes@samspublishing.com

249

How can we make this index more useful? Email us at indexes@samspublishing.com

251

How can we make this index more useful? Email us at indexes@samspublishing.com

253

INDEX

How can we make this index more useful? Email us at indexes@samspublishing.com

255

How can we make this index more useful? Email us at indexes@samspublishing.com

257

INDEX

How can we make this index more useful? Email us at indexes@samspublishing.com

259

T

How can we make this index more useful? Email us at indexes@samspublishing.com

261